Becoming God's True Woman

...WHILE I STILL HAVE A CURFEW

Becoming God's True Woman

...WHILE I STILL HAVE A CURFEW

SUSAN HUNT
MARY A. KASSIAN

MOODY PUBLISHERS
CHICAGO

All Scripture quotations, unless otherwise indicated, are taken from *The Holy Bible, English Standard Version.* Copyright © 2000, 2001 by Crossway Bibles, a division of Good News Publishers. Used by permission. All rights reserved.

Scripture quotations marked HCSB are taken from *The Holman Christian Standard Bible* © 2001, Broadman & Holman Publishers, Lifeway Christian Resources, 127 Ninth Avenue North, Nashville, Tennessee 37234. All rights reserved.

Scriptures marked NIV are take from *The Holy Bible, New International Version*®. NIV®. Copyright © 1973, 1978, 1984, 2011 by Biblica, Inc.™ Used by permission. All rights reserved worldwide.

Scriptures marked NIV 1984 taken from *The Holy Bible, New International Version*®. Copyright © 1973, 1978, 1984 Biblica, Inc.™ Used by permission of Zondervan. All rights reserved worldwide. www.zondervan.com

Scriptures marked NKJV are taken from *The New King James Version.* Copyright 1982 by Thomas Nelson, Inc. Used by permission. All rights reserved.

Edited by Jeanette Gardner Littleton
Interior and Cover design: www.DesignByJulia.com with inspiration from Mary A. Kassian
Cover image: Magone / Shutterstock
Mary Kasian Photo: Photography by Katie
Susan Hunt Photo: JD3 Photo

Library of Congress Cataloging-in-Publication Data

Hunt, Susan, 1940-
  Becoming God's true woman-- while I still have a curfew / Susan Hunt, Mary A. Kassian.
     p. cm.
  ISBN 978-0-8024-0360-5
1. Women--Religious aspects--Christianity--Textbooks. 2. Women--Biblical teaching--Textbooks. I. Kassian, Mary A. II. Title.
  BT704.H855 2012
  248.8'43--dc23
                          2012020940

We hope you enjoy this book from Moody Publishers. Our goal is to provide high-quality, thought-provoking books and products that connect truths to your real needs and challenges. For more information on other books and products written and produced from a biblical perspective, go to www.moodypublishers.com or write to:

Moody Publishers
820 N. LaSalle Boulevard
Chicago, IL 60610

1 3 5 7 9 10 8 6 4 2

Printed in the United States of America

Letter from Susan

Dear Covenant Daughter,

I may not know you and I may never meet you, but I love you.

My husband and I have twelve grandchildren—six granddaughters and six grandsons. As I write this they range in age from five to twenty-one, so I probably have a grandchild your age. They call me Memommy. I go to soccer, basketball, baseball, football, and softball games, graduations, and recitals. Our grandkids have taught me to text. I love your generation!

As I think about your generation, my prayer is from Psalm 71:18:

So even to old age and gray hairs, O God, do not forsake me, until I proclaim your might to another generation, your power to all those to come.

One of the things I want to tell your generation is that learning true womanhood—womanhood that reflects the truth of the gospel—is the only way to experience true peace and joy.

I want our granddaughters and spiritual granddaughters (that means you) to know this because I want you to be true women who live for God's glory.

I want our grandsons to know this because I want them to marry a true woman.

Mary Kassian and I have had a great time working together on these devotions. In Part 1, I share some basic biblical principles of womanhood, and in Part 2, Mary gives some practical implications of these principles.

Scattered throughout Part 1 are stories written by girls and women sharing their testimonies of their teen years. I am deeply grateful to each of these and inspired by their stories of God's grace. I think you will be too.

Mary and I pray that the Lord will use these devotions to shape you into a true woman who thinks, prays, and lives for His glory.

Susan

I There Is a Difference

M ale and female . . . fascinating!

Have you ever wondered why God created people in His image?

Have you thought about His purpose for you as a female?

Have you considered the fact that God intentionally planned everything about your life?

So God created man in his own image, in the image of God he created him; male and female he created them.

GENESIS 1:27

Consider these jaw-dropping words from Acts 17:26: "And he made from one man every nation of mankind to live on all the face of the earth, having determined allotted periods and the boundaries of their dwelling place."

Think about it: God determined the "allotted period"—the exact time in history when you would live.

He determined the boundaries—the exact place on the planet where you would live.

He determined the family, friends, and circumstances of your life.

And He determined that you would be a female.

How extraordinary!

After God created the man and woman He said that this creation was very good.

It really is.

Will you join us on a journey to explore our very good calling to true womanhood?

After each devotion you will find suggestions to help you learn to think, pray, and live for God's glory. I encourage you to spend time journaling your journey. You may want to read the devotion one day and journal the next day, or read all the devotions, and then re-read them and do the "Time for You" sections. To help you get started, I asked our teen granddaughters to write their thoughts. Read what they said, and then it will be your turn.

Time to THINK

Write your thoughts and feelings about Acts 17:26.

"This scripture makes me feel like I shouldn't complain or be unhappy with things in my life because God put these in place on purpose. It also gives me confidence that He is in control. God put all the people who are in my life there for a reason. Sometimes life is hard, but I know God has a plan for me. He made me in His own image, and He sacrificed His Son for me. I am grateful that He has a good plan for my life. I want to keep worshiping and praising Him."—Suzie, age 15

Time to PRAY

Write a prayer using Genesis 1:27 and Acts 17:26.

"Dear Jesus, thank you for creating me in Your image. Thank You for giving me a loving family and Christian friends. Thank You for having a plan for my life. Please help me glorify You in all that I do. In Jesus' name, amen."—Cassie, age 14

"Dear God, thank You for all Your blessings, specifically for what You did in creation, designing us humans as male and female, both equally good in Your image. It is so comforting to know, like You say in Acts, that You already know my every situation and surrounding, that nothing surprises You, that You have everything under control, and that You specifically made me a woman—a woman who strives to be true. I pray that You will help me every day to become more and more like a true woman and to honor You in all my endeavors and in my role as a woman. In Your name I pray, amen."—Mary Kate, age 19

Suzie, Cassie, and Mary Kate had their time— now it's time for you to write your thoughts.

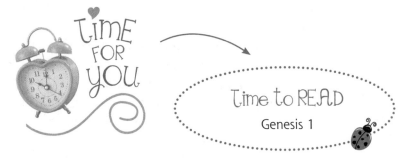

Time for You

Time to READ
Genesis 1

Time to THINK

Think about Acts 17:26. God planned when and where you would live, and the people and circumstances of your life. Write your thoughts and feelings about this incredible reality.

_____

_____

_____

_____

Time to PRAY

Using God's Word as the basis for our praise and petitions helps us to know God and His Word more intimately. It deepens our prayer life. Write a prayer using Genesis 1:27 and Acts 17:26.

_____

_____

_____

_____

Time to LIVE FOR GOD'S GLORY

Tell someone what you learned from Genesis 1:27 and Acts 17:26.

The Big Story

2

The Bible is not simply a collection of disconnected stories and events. It is one big story of God keeping His promise to redeem His people. "To redeem" means to pay a ransom. The Bible is the story of Jesus, the Redeemer, who came and lived among us and gave His life as the ransom to free us from sin.

> I will make my dwelling among you . . . And I will walk among you and will be your God, and you shall be my people.
>
> LEVITICUS 26:11–12

Womanhood is part of this story of redemption. We will never understand our womanhood unless we see it as part of this amazing story that begins before the beginning.

Ephesians 1 gives a glimpse into what happened before creation:

"Blessed be the God and Father of our Lord Jesus Christ, who has blessed us in Christ with every spiritual blessing in the heavenly places, even as he chose us in him before the foundation of the world . . . In love he predestined us for adoption as sons through Jesus Christ, according to the purpose of his will, to the praise of his glorious grace . . . " (vv. 3–6).

"In him [Jesus] we have redemption through his blood, the forgiveness of our trespasses . . . so that we who were the first to hope in Christ might be to the praise of his glory" (7, 12).

"In him you also . . . were sealed with the promised Holy Spirit, who is the guarantee of our inheritance until we acquire possession of it, to the praise of his glory (vv. 13–14).

Here we see an agreement, a covenant, between the members of the Trinity. In this agreement each Person of the Trinity assumed a different function.

- Look at verses 3–6 again. What did God the Father agree to do for us?

- Look at verses 7–12. What did Jesus agree to do for us?

- Look at verses 13–14. What did the Holy Spirit agree to do for us?

God the Father chose us to be His children before He created the world. He did not choose us because of anything we would be or do. He chose us because of His love.

God the Son agreed to give His life to redeem God's people from sin. He agreed to pay the redemption price by dying on the cross as punishment for our sin.

God the Holy Spirit agreed to give God's people the power to believe that the Father chose us and the Son died for us. He is the guarantee that we will receive the fullness of the benefits of redemption when Jesus comes back.

This agreement between the Father, Son, and Holy Spirit is called the covenant of redemption. Each Person of the Trinity has a different function in this covenant, but the goal is the same. What is God's overriding goal of His redemption plan? Look again at verses 6, 12, and 14. Underline the recurring phrase.

The Father chose us, the Son redeems us, and the Holy Spirit gives us the power to believe the gospel message so that we can praise His glorious grace.

Grace is God's gift—Jesus—to us. We can do nothing to deserve or earn this gift. Grace is also His power—the Holy Spirit—in us. The redemption story is the story of God's grace.

This is the big story, and you are part of it.

Q. **Which Person of the Trinity is most important for our salvation?**

A. The Father, Son, and Holy Spirit are equal, and the function of each Person in the Trinity is equal, but these functions are different. Equal but different—what an intriguing concept.

Time FOR you

Time to THINK

Personalize the verses above by putting your own name in them. For example:
"I will give Susan a heart to know that I am the Lord, and she shall be my child and I will be her God, for she shall return to me with her whole heart" (Jeremiah 24:7). Next, write your thoughts about this extraordinary promise.

Time to READ

These verses are just a few places where we read God's promise to be our God. Read several of them.

Genesis 17:7 ▪ Exodus 6:7 ▪ Jeremiah 24:7
▪ 2 Corinthians 6:16 ▪ Revelation 21:1–4

Time to PRAY

Use the verses you read and write a prayer of gratitude to God.

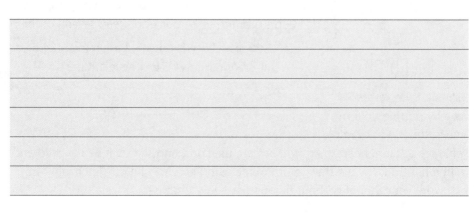

Time to LIVE FOR GOD'S GLORY

Think about the Triune God's promise that He will be your God and you will be His child. Think of one difference that being God's child should make in your life and write it down. Then ask the Holy Spirit to change your heart so that you want to live as God's daughter.

Dianne's Story

Patty approached me one Sunday at church. She was pretty and outgoing, and I was flattered that she would talk with me.

"Your mom said you may be interested in coming to our youth Bible study on Wednesdays," she said.

"That sounds great," I lied. I had no intention of going to church twice in one week.

By Wednesday I had forgotten the conversation, but Patty remembered. She called me, and when I answered the telephone, her bright voice on the other end of the line said, "We're all here. Where are you?"

I reluctantly drove to the house where they were meeting, and Patty warmly welcomed me.

There I encountered something I had never experienced: Teenage girls were worshiping the Lord. These girls were my age, yet they talked to God as if He was in that very room. I was captivated. I was overwhelmed with an intense desire to have that kind of relationship with God.

Patty sat beside me as I discovered Christ as my personal Savior. After I prayed and asked Jesus to be part of my life, Patty explained to me how a person grows closer to God through daily Bible reading and prayer. I was moved by her concern for me. But I was even more moved by her love for Jesus.

Patty persevered. The next day she called me to see if I had any questions about my decision to follow Jesus. I did have some questions, so she invited me to spend the night at her home. Patty loved God so much that I expected her to have a whole family of people who were strong Christians, so I was surprised to learn that Patty was the only one in her home who had a relationship with God. We spent hours in her room talking, praying, and praising God.

The years have passed. My husband and I have spent over twenty years on the mission field. I lost contact with Patty, but I have not forgotten her. Many times I think of Patty and wish I could tell her what an encouragement she was to me. The faithfulness to God she showed when she was eighteen still challenges me today.

Dianne Smalling, Missionary

(This story is adapted from TRUE, a discipleship curriculum for teen girls. Used by permission.)

Equal but Different

You have probably heard this joke: God created man and said, "I can do better than that," and He created woman.

> Male and female he created them, and he blessed them and named them Man when they were created.
>
> GENESIS 5:2

While you might laugh, I hope you see that this joke isn't true. God did exactly what He intended to do—He created male and female, and He declared the idea of two genders to be very good.

You have probably heard another untruth: Equality means females must do the same thing as males.

Two things do not have to be the same to be equal. Red and green are equally colors, but they are different.

God created male and female, and He created them equally in His image. However He gave them different functions in His kingdom. These functions are equally valuable.

Does this sound familiar?

- The Father, Son, and Holy Spirit are equal.

- Each Person of the Trinity has a different function in accomplishing our redemption.

- These different functions have the same purpose— to praise the Triune God's glorious grace.

- There is *equality* in being, *difference* in function, and *unity* in purpose.

The same is true for us because we were created in the likeness of the Triune God.

- Men and women are equal because we are both created in God's image. Neither is more important nor more valuable than the other.

- We were designed for different functions.

- We were created for the same purpose: God's glory.

- There is *equality* in being, *difference* in function, and *unity* in purpose.

It's nonsense to say that God the Father must die on the cross in order to be as important as the Son, and it is nonsense to say that women must do the same things as men in order to be as important.

Men and women are different, but our differences are not meant to divide us— and they won't if we have the same purpose. The problem is when our purpose is to live for our own glory rather than God's glory.

God's plan is for men and women to live in harmony and to praise Him together. We are not to compete and criticize. We are to value our differences. We are to encourage and help each other glorify God.

The big story that began before the beginning, and that runs through history, is the story of God redeeming His people by sending His Son to be our Savior and by giving His Spirit to us so that we can believe this amazing salvation story and live for His glory.

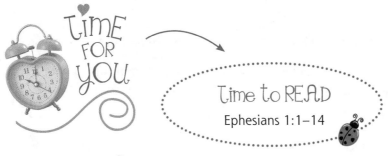

Time to THINK

What are your thoughts about the Triune God's plan and purpose
that we see in Ephesians 1:1–14?

_____

_____

_____

_____

Have you trusted Jesus to be your Savior? If so, reflect on God's
amazing grace in your life.

_____

_____

_____

_____

What are your thoughts about Dianne's Story?

_____

_____

_____

_____

Time to PRAY

Use Ephesians 1:1–14 to write your prayer.

Time to LIVE FOR GOD'S GLORY

If you are trusting Jesus to be your Savior, it is because God chose you to belong to Him before He created the world. What difference should this make in how you live?

Same Purpose

4

guys and girls have the same purpose.

You both have dignity and worth because you were created in God's image.

> Then God said,
> "Let us make man in our image, after our likeness."
> GENESIS 1:26

Your value is not determined by your abilities, your looks, or your popularity. You are valuable because you are God's image-bearer.

Being God's image-bearer means that we were created to live in a special relationship with Him and to reflect some of His wonderful characteristics.

Think of it this way:

When you look into a mirror you see a reflection, or an image, of yourself. The reflection does not show everything about you, but it does show some things about you. When the mirror is turned away from you, it does not reflect you. The mirror reflects what it faces. When we live in relationship with God through Christ, we reflect His glory; when we turn away, we do not.

God created us in His image so we can reflect some things about Him. We do not show everything about Him, but we were created to reflect some aspects of His glory.

A catechism is a method of teaching by questions and answers.
I will use some questions from historic catechisms that have been used
by the church for centuries to teach biblical doctrine.

Westminster Shorter Catechism

Q. 1: **What is the chief end of man?**

A: Man's chief end is to glorify God, and to enjoy him forever.

The Heidelberg Catechism

Q. 6: **Did God create people so wicked and perverse?**

A: No. God created them good and in His own image, that is,
in true righteousness and holiness, so that they might truly know
God their creator, love Him with all their heart, and live with Him
in eternal happiness for His praise and glory.

The true woman's purpose is to glorify God. For the record, the true man's purpose is also to glorify God.

The true woman does not live for herself. She does not seek her own honor. Instead, no matter what she does, her purpose is to reflect God's glory. She embraces 1 Corinthians 10:31: "So, whether you eat or drink, or whatever you do, do all to the glory of God."

> *"Turn my heart toward your statutes and not toward selfish gain, Turn my eyes away from worthless things; preserve my life according to your word."*
>
> (PSALM 119:36–37, NIV)

The girl who wants to become a true woman will continually ask God to turn her to Himself so that she will reflect His glory.

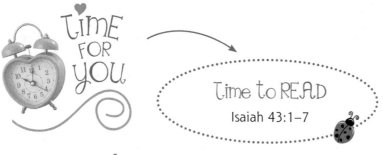

Time FOR you

Time to READ

Isaiah 43:1–7

Time to THINK

Read Isaiah 43:1–7 again and substitute your name for Jacob and Israel. What are your thoughts about this incredible passage? What is your purpose? Do you really want to live for God's glory, or do you want to live for yourself?

Time to PRAY

Use 1 Corinthians 10:31 to write your prayer. Include some of the specific things that you do such as schoolwork and playing soccer, and ask the Lord for grace to do it for His glory.

Time to LIVE FOR GOD'S GLORY

Memorize the answer to the Catechism question: What is the chief end of man? Man's chief end is to glorify God, and to enjoy Him forever.

Substitute your name for "Man's" and write it on an index card. Put it where you will see it every day (maybe on your mirror!).

The Moon's Story

We sat on the beach dazzled by the sights and sounds. Moonbeams danced on the water. Waves crashed onto the shore, and a full moon hung above us.

"Children," I whispered to the grandkids sitting on the blanket, "God's Word says, 'The heavens declare the glory of God; the skies proclaim the work of his hands' [Psalm 19:1, NIV]. Do you hear what the sky is telling us?"

Silence.

I asked them to look at the moon and describe it.

"It's big," declared the six-year-old.

"It's beautiful," sighed the nine-year-old.

"That's it," I said. "God is big, and He's beautiful. That's the moon's message to us. But did you know that the moon has no light of its own?"

The six-year-old protested, "But it's shining!"

The fifteen-year-old explained, "It reflects light from the sun."

"Then why don't we have a full moon every night?" I asked.

The clever twelve-year-old was ready. "Because the moon has to be lined up with the sun in exactly the right position."

"I get it!" exclaimed the sixteen-year-old breathlessly. "We're like the moon. We have no light of our own. We reflect God's light."

"But we must be in exactly the right position. We must be fully facing Him," reflected a wise nineteen-year-old.

"When we live facing Jesus, we reflect His glorious goodness—and it's dazzling," said a satisfied grandma.

A Good Question

5

A teen girl asked an interesting question.

"Wasn't it . . . well, I mean . . ." she hesitated, not sure if she should verbalize her question.

"It's all right," I said. "Honest questions are good. How will we learn if we don't ask?"

She began again, "Wasn't it egotistical of God to create us for His glory? That seems self-serving."

"That's a thoughtful question that deserves an answer," I replied. "But first let me ask you a question. What other purpose could we have that would give us more significance than glorifying God?"

She thought for a while and finally said, "I can't think of anything."

She could not think of anything because there is nothing more significant than being created to live in relationship with the King of kings, the Creator and Sustainer of the universe, and to reflect certain aspects of His goodness.

> All the nations you have made shall come and worship before you, O Lord, and shall glorify your name.
>
> PSALM 86:9

make no mistake—God does not need us in order to be glorious.

God is glorious whether we glorify Him or not. He graciously created us in His image so that we can glorify Him. All of creation reflects the glory of His beauty, power, and majesty, but humans are the ones He created to live in such a personal relationship with Him that we can reflect the glory of His character.

Not only does living for His praise and honor give us significance, it is the only thing that gives us joy. This is what we were created for and anything less dishonors God and demeans us.

The psalmist cried out in Psalm 8:1, 4–5, "O Lord, our Lord, how majestic is your name in all the earth! You have set your glory above the heavens . . . what is man that you are mindful of him, . . . you have . . . crowned him with glory and honor."

And in Psalm 86:12, "I give thanks to you, O Lord my God, with my whole heart, and I will glorify your name forever."

Paul wrote in 1 Corinthians 6:19–20, "Do you not know that your body is a temple of the Holy Spirit within you, whom you have from God? You are not your own, for you were bought with a price. So glorify God in your body."

The girl who is becoming a true woman continually asks herself questions such as:

- What will it mean for me to glorify God in this relationship or situation?

- How can I glorify God in my family?

- How can I glorify God as a student?

- How can I glorify God in my choices of everything from clothes to college?

The girl who is becoming a true woman knows that God created us for His glory because He loves us. Her gratitude for such love causes her to sing with the angels, "Glory to God in the highest, and on earth peace among those with whom he is pleased!" (Luke 2:14).

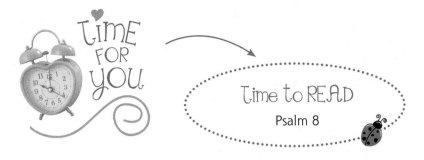

Time to READ

Psalm 8

Time to THINK

Write your thoughts about God creating you for His glory.

What are your thoughts about The Moon's Story?

Time to PRAY

Use the Scriptures on pages 24–25 to write your prayer.

Time to LIVE FOR GOD'S GLORY

Develop the holy habit of asking yourself the questions a true woman asks. Start by asking one of the questions and writing your answer. Then pray for God's power to do it.

6 Same Authority

The authority and power of God's Word brought creation into existence. He spoke and it happened. God said for light to appear and light appeared.

He spoke and the world immediately obeyed.

God's Word is the authority for every molecule in the universe. His Word is the authority for every male and female, whether we recognize it or not.

God has given us the Bible so that we may know Him and know how to glorify Him.

What the true woman believes and how she lives is not determined by her opinions, feelings, or desires. What she believes and how she lives is determined by God's Word.

God's Word is the authority for all of life. In fact, His Word is our life.

In Deuteronomy 32:46–47 NIV, Moses stressed the importance of God's words to the Israelites by telling them,

> In the beginning, God created the heavens and the earth . . . And God said, "Let there be light," and there was light.
>
> GENESIS 1:1, 3

Westminster Shorter Catechism

Q. 2: **What rule hath God given to direct us how we may glorify and enjoy him?**

A: The Word of God, which is contained in the Scriptures of the Old and New Testaments, is the only rule to direct us how we may glorify and enjoy him.

"Take to heart all the words I have solemnly declared to you this day, so that you may command your children to obey carefully all the words of this law. They are not just idle words for you—they are your life."

Jesus said, "Man shall not live by bread alone, but by every word that comes from the mouth of God" (Matthew 4:4).

The words that the world tells us are not words of life. The words of the world are worthless.

The words of the world tell us to do what makes us happy even if it means disobeying our parents.

God's Word says: "Children, obey your parents in everything, for this pleases the Lord" (Colossians 3:20).

The words of the world tell us to get revenge on those who hurt us.

God's Word says: "Love your enemies and pray for those who persecute you" (Matthew 5:44).

The words of the world tell us that money and stuff will make us happy, so get all you can.

God's Word says: "Keep your life free from love of money, and be content with what you have, for he has said, '"I will never leave you nor forsake you"'" (Hebrews 13:5).

When we first read it, God's Word may seem radical and is shocking to our self-centered hearts. And not only is it shocking, it is impossible to follow.

A girl who wants to become a true woman knows she cannot obey God's Word in her own strength. She asks God to give her His power to love and obey His Word. She prays that He will turn her away from the worthless things and turn her to the Worthy One.

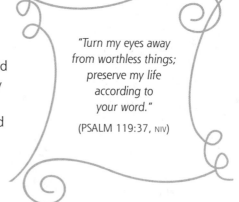

"Turn my eyes away from worthless things; preserve my life according to your word."

(PSALM 119:37, NIV)

Time FOR YOU

Time to READ

Psalm 19:7–14

Time to THINK

What is your authority? Does God's Word determine your attitudes and actions, or do your feelings and desires rule you? Write your thoughts.

Time to PRAY

Use Psalm 119:37 and write a prayer. Name some of the specific worthless things that tempt you and ask God for grace to turn from them.

Time to LIVE FOR GOD'S GLORY

Memorize Psalm 119:37 and make it your prayer every morning.

Leigh's Story

I have wonderful childhood memories: from swimming in the backyard with my brother and sister to playing competitive softball. I was blessed with a loving Christian family. But, when I was fifteen, my mother was diagnosed with a brain stem tumor and my world turned upside down.

Doctors removed the tumor, but the surgery left my mom in a wheelchair permanently. Seeing my mother's health change so dramatically broke me, but God's sovereignty and unconditional love found me. He comforted me by His mercy and guided me by His sovereign grace. He became my compass, refuge, and strength.

After Mom's surgery, life at home changed. I quickly realized how much we had relied on her. She was the one who cooked, cleaned, did laundry, and bought groceries. Her to-do list never ended. She had done so much for us, and I knew it was my turn to help out. I didn't have much time for hanging out with friends or dating.

I graduated from high school and was accepted into Auburn University. I thought college would be a break from some of the responsibilities, but after one semester I knew my place wasn't at Auburn. God wanted me closer to home to help my family.

The Lord provided an amazing opportunity for me to transfer to a junior college near my home, where I was offered a full athletic scholarship! When I graduated from there He provided a second athletic scholarship to Reinhardt University (also close to home). I had a blast at Reinhardt—making lifelong friends, playing softball, and even meeting my husband there.

Looking back, I'm amazed at God's grace and love for me. He carried me through the pain and struggles while teaching me to glorify and trust Him in my circumstances. He unveiled His path beneath my feet, revealed His divine plan for me, gave me a heart to obey Him, and guided me in each step of my teenage journey. He still does as I'm learning to be a wife and mother for His glory.

Leigh Prather, Powder Springs, Georgia

Different Design

men and women have the same authority and the same purpose, but they have different designs.

> The Lord God said, "It is not good that the man should be alone; I will make him a helper fit for him."
>
> GENESIS 2:18

God did not say that the man was not good. He said that man's aloneness was not good.

Why wasn't aloneness good? Because the man was created in the image of God, and the Father, Son, and Holy Spirit live in a perfect relationship of love. The man needed a relationship with one who was equal, but different, so that together they could glorify God. The different designs were intended to harmonize to reflect the unity and diversity of the Triune God.

Perhaps you cringe a bit at the word "helper"—or maybe you cringe a lot! Helper might seem at first to be an inferior role. But let's look more closely at how this word is used in Scripture.

The Hebrew word (the Old Testament was written in Hebrew) for helper—ezer—is often used to refer to God as our Helper, so obviously being a helper does not mean we are less important than the person being helped. Knowing how God is our Helper gives us insight into what it means to be a helper.

Here are a few examples.

- He defends: Moses said, "My father's God was my helper; he saved me from the sword of Pharaoh" (Exodus 18:4 NIV).

- He sees and cares for suffering: "But you, O God, do see trouble and grief; you consider it to take it in hand. The victim commits himself to you; you are the helper of the fatherless" (Psalm 10:14 NIV 1984).

- He supports: "May he send you help from the sanctuary and grant you support from Zion" (Psalm 20:2 NIV).

- He protects: "We wait in hope for the Lord; he is our help and our shield" (Psalm 33:20 NIV).

- He delivers from distress: "Yet I am poor and needy; come quickly to me, O God. You are my help and my deliverer; O Lord, do not delay" (Psalm 70:5 NIV 1984).

- He rescues: "For he will deliver the needy who cry out, the afflicted who have no one to help. He will take pity on the weak and the needy and save the needy from death. He will rescue them from oppression and violence, for precious is their blood in his sight" (Psalm 72:12–14 NIV).

- He comforts: "You, O Lord, have helped me and comforted me" (Psalm 86:17 NIV 1984).

These are not wimpy words. They are strong, relational, caring, nurturing words. God designed His female creation to give warmth, compassion, and support to relationships.

God's female design is spectacular. So are you when you fulfill this design.

This is what God designed the woman to be and do, and she was perfectly happy glorifying God as a helper until she listened to the evil one.

Q: **Yikes! Does this mean a wife is supposed to help her husband do anything he wants her to do?**

A: Absolutely not! She is to help him glorify God. She is not to help him sin.

Time for YOU

Time to READ
John 14:15–17

Time to THINK

According to John 14:15–17, who is our Helper? Summarize these verses in your own words.

What are your thoughts about Leigh's Story?

Time to PRAY

Use John 14:15–17 to write your prayer.

Time to LIVE FOR GOD'S GLORY

Select one of the helper words (defends, supports, etc.), and think about how to apply it to one of your relationships. For example: A friend criticizes your parents because they won't let you go to a party. How do you defend your parents' reputation and decision?

8

Same Sin

....

The creation drama in Genesis 1 and 2 moves so quickly that our heads spin. Light appears . . . then land . . . plants . . . sea creatures . . . birds . . . animals. Then, wonder of wonders—an image-bearer of the Creator. Then, wonder added to wonder—a female version!

It's easy to get so caught up in this breathtaking drama that we miss the defining moment for the rest of history.

Genesis 2:15–17 says, "The Lord God took the man and put him in the garden of Eden to work it and keep it. And the Lord God commanded the man, saying, 'You may surely eat of every tree of the garden, but of the tree of the knowledge of good and evil you shall not eat, for in the day that you eat of it you shall surely die.'"

The destiny of those who would follow hinged on Adam. He represented us all. Obedience meant life; disobedience meant death. It still does.

Then God said it was not good for the man to be alone. God paraded the animals before the man, and Adam named them. The privilege and responsibility of naming shows the man's function of headship—that he was over the other created beings.

None of the animals were what Adam needed. He needed one who was equal to him, but different. Then God created the woman—exactly what God planned and Adam needed.

Did God actually say . . . ?

GENESIS 3:1

In Genesis 3:1 the dark side of the story begins: "Now the serpent was more crafty than any other beast of the field that the Lord God had made. He said to the woman, 'Did God actually say, "You shall not eat of any tree in the garden"?'"

The man and woman ate the forbidden fruit. They rebelled against God's authority. They turned away from Him. They wanted to be their own authority and to seek their own honor rather than obey God's Word and live for His glory. Sin entered the world, and all who would follow would be sinners—every male and female. Romans 3:22–23 explains, "For there is no distinction: for all have sinned and fall short of the glory of God."

When the man and woman rejected God's authority they lost their relationship with Him, and as a result, they lost their ability to glorify Him. They lost their ability to be and do what they were created to be and do. The woman lost her ability to be a helper.

The true woman became a new woman.

- The true woman's purpose is God's glory, and her authority is God's Word.

- The new woman's purpose is her glory, and her authority is her own word.

Sin brought death. There was immediate spiritual death—separation from God. And the bodies of the man and woman began the process of aging and death.

"For the wages of sin is death, but . . . " (Romans 6:23).

The story should have ended there, with death, but it didn't.

· ·

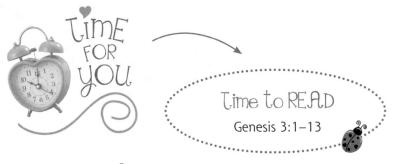

Time for You

Time to READ
Genesis 3:1–13

Time to THINK

What did we lose because of sin?

Satan tempted the man and woman to question God's authority.
How are you tempted to rebel against God's Word?

Time to PRAY

Pray Psalm 139:23–24: "Search me, O God, and know my heart! Try me and know my thoughts! And see if there be any grievous way in me, and lead me in the way everlasting!"

Time to LIVE FOR GOD'S GLORY

What is one sinful attitude or action that is hard for you to resist or overcome? Write it down and ask your Helper to help you turn from it.

Same Gospel

9

Why didn't God end all His plans for humans and earth when the man and woman sinned? Because God is a covenant keeper. Before creation the Father, Son, and Holy Spirit covenanted, or made a solemn agreement, to redeem His people. Nothing could stop Him from keeping this promise.

> For the wages of sin is death, but the free gift of God is eternal life in Christ Jesus our Lord.
>
> ROMANS 6:23

The man and woman listened as God said to the serpent: "And I will put enmity between you and the woman, and between your offspring and hers; he will crush your head, and you will strike his heel" (Genesis 3:15 NIV).

- "Enmity" means hostility. The man and woman could not free themselves from Satan's grip no matter what they did, but God said He would rescue them.

- The woman would have children. That meant life and not death.

- One would come who would be wounded for them but would win the victory over sin and death.

- The One who would come would be an offspring of the woman.

Genesis 3:15 is the first proclamation of the gospel, which means "good news."

We may have a hard time imagining how good the good news was for the man and woman. They heard the curse God pronounced upon Satan—his head would be crushed. They watched him slither away. Surely they wondered what would happen to them now. They knew they deserved the same kind of curse Satan received, but they both heard the same gospel.

....

The Westminster Shorter Catechism

Q. 20 : **Did God leave all mankind to perish in the estate of sin and misery?**

A: God having, out of his mere good pleasure, from all eternity, elected some to everlasting life, did enter into a covenant of grace, to deliver them out of the estate of sin and misery, and to bring them into an estate of salvation by a Redeemer.

Q. 21 : **Who is the Redeemer of God's elect?**

A: The only Redeemer of God's elect is the Lord Jesus Christ, who, being the eternal Son of God, became man and so was, and continueth to be, God and man in two distinct natures, and one person, forever.

....

Disobedience means death. Obedience means life. But now Another would obey in the place of those the Father chose before creation.

Adam failed as the representative of God's people, but God's promise meant there would be a new Representative for God's people.

Romans 5:12, 19 explains: "Therefore, just as sin came into the world through one man, and death through sin, and so death spread to all men because all sinned . . . For as by the one man's [Adam's] disobedience the many were made sinners, so by the one man's [Christ's] obedience the many will be made righteous."

The Father promised to send the Son, who would obey God and restore the relationship with God that Adam lost because of his disobedience. This is called a covenant of grace because the man and woman could do nothing to earn this gift. They didn't deserve this, but received it anyway!

God saves us not because we deserve it but because of His amazing love.

....

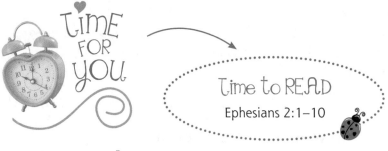

TiME FOR YOU

Time to READ
Ephesians 2:1–10

Time to THINK

Read Ephesians 2:1–10 and substitute "I" and "me" for "you" and "we."

According to this passage what is our condition without Christ?

What is our condition in Christ?

Why does God give us life (v. 4)?

Read the following verses and write your thoughts about God's love for you.
■ Deuteronomy 7:6–8 ■ John 3:16 ■ Romans 5:8 ■ I John 3:1

_____

_____

_____

_____

_____

Time to PRAY

Use Ephesians 2:1–10 to write your prayer.

_____

_____

_____

_____

_____

Time to LIVE FOR GOD'S GLORY

What is your response to such amazing love?
What difference should Ephesians 2:1–10 make in
your attitudes and actions?

_____

_____

_____

_____

Womanhood Redeemed

10

What was Adam's response to the good news? He gave the woman a name, and it was a name with great significance: Eve.

> Adam named his wife Eve, because she would become the mother of all the living.
>
> GENESIS 3:20 NIV

"Eve" means "life-giver." This name shows Adam's belief in the gospel promise—the promise of life, not death. It points to Jesus, the One who would bring life to the world. It celebrates the goodness of this good news.

Eve's name also celebrates woman's mission. Womanhood was redeemed. Being a life-giver is not just biological—though our ability to give birth is stunning. The redeemed female—regardless of age—has the ability to be a life-giver in every relationship and situation because the life of Christ is in her. She has the ability to do the good work of being a helper that God prepared for her to do.

If Christ is your Savior, you have the potential to be a life-giver, but our own sin and the influence of culture tempt us to be life-takers.

Think about your words. Do they give life to others or do they hurt others? Proverbs 18:21 is clear: "Death and life are in the power of the tongue" (Proverbs 18:21).

Think about your relationships. Do you give life to them or do you suck the life out of them? Do you help or hurt others? Consider this contrast between the True Woman and the New Woman. Although these Scriptures actually refer to God, as true women wanting to be like Him, in His image, we can apply them to our own lives.

The True Woman	The New Woman
Helper/Life-giver	*Hinderer/Life-taker*
Ex. 18:4, Defends	Attacks
Ps. 10:14, Sees, cares for oppressed	Indifferent, unconcerned for oppressed
Ps. 20:2, Supports	Weakens
Ps. 33:20, Shields, protects	Leaves unprotected
Ps. 70:5, Delivers from distress	Causes distress
Ps. 72:12–14, Rescues poor, weak, needy	Ignores poor, weak, needy
Ps. 86:17 Comforts	Causes discomfort

Becoming a life-giver—a true woman—is a lifelong process. Only fearless females can aspire to this calling, but it takes more than courage. It takes the power of the gospel to transform us from life-takers to life-givers. Becoming a life-giver means dying to self so that the life of Christ fills us and flows from us. Read and reflect on the following scriptures:

"We know that our old self was crucified with him in order that the body of sin might be brought to nothing, so that we would no longer be enslaved to sin . . . So you also must consider yourselves dead to sin and alive to God in Christ Jesus" (Romans 6:6, 11).

"He himself bore our sins in his body on the tree, that we might die to sin and live to righteousness. By his wounds you have been healed" (1 Peter 2:24).

"He [Jesus] must increase, but I must decrease" (John 3:30).

And get this—redeemed females are the only ones on the planet who can show the dazzling beauty of God's female design to a dying world because only redeemed women have true life.

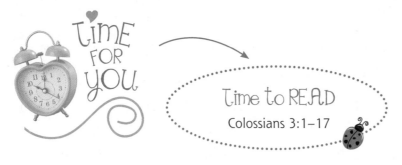

Time for You

Time to READ
Colossians 3:1–17

Time to THINK

According to Colossians 3:1–17 what are some things you should put off and put on?

Put off (life-taker), vv. 5–10	Put on (life-giver), vv. 12–17

Time to PRAY

Pray for grace to be a life-giver by putting off and putting on.

Time to LIVE FOR GOD'S GLORY

Practice Colossians 3:17: Do everything in the name of Christ—by His power and for His glory—with gratitude to the Father.

Gratitude's Story

My friend Karen emailed me this: "Before bedtime I write things I'm thankful for from that day: a warm bed, my loving husband lying beside me, lunch with a friend, a finished project, a conversation that strengthened a relationship, the snow. I thank the Lord for these undeserved gifts. I started this to develop gratitude and fight a selfish heart. I've been surprised that my quality of sleep has improved!"

Do you have a grateful heart or a grumbling heart?

Life-givers are grateful. Life-takers are grumblers.

A grateful heart is humble. A grumbling heart is selfish. A grateful heart is focused on God's goodness and love. A grumbling heart is focused on self.

When Jesus makes our dead hearts alive, we have the ability to be grateful. Gratitude is a life-giving grace.

Psalm 100:4 tells us: "Enter his gates with thanksgiving, and his courts with praise! Give thanks to him; bless his name!"

Gratitude is the gateway to God's presence. We are to approach Him with thankfulness. An ungrateful heart keeps us from God!

Let's experiment together. Let's develop the holy habit of gratitude. Beginning with the next "It's Your Time" section, you will be asked to write at least one thing you are grateful for.

The True or the New

The words that describe a helper are action words: defends, sees, and cares for the oppressed, supports, shields, and protects, delivers from distress, rescues the poor and weak, and comforts.

> Keep your heart with all vigilance, for from it flow the springs of life.
>
> PROVERBS 4:23

This is what a true woman does.

Before sin entered the world these actions came naturally because the woman lived facing God. The true woman's mind and heart were not polluted with sin. Now, even though we are redeemed and the life of Christ is in us, we still struggle with sin—our own, the sin of others that hurts us, and the sin of a fallen world that tempts us.

When Adam named the woman he did not use some form of ezer, the word for helper. He used a name that points to the gospel: life. Rather than emphasizing what a woman does, this name emphasizes what we are given.

Our actions can be deceptive. They can deceive us and others.

For instance, you can defend the reputation of your friend by correcting lies someone says about her, but why are you doing it? Is it because you have a heart that cares about truth and justice? Or do you defend her so she won't tell lies about you?

You can help the needy by volunteering in a homeless shelter, but are you doing it because God has filled your heart with compassion for the poor? Or to pad your resume for college?

Do you support your parents by obeying their rules because you want to obey God's Word and honor your parents? Or so they won't ground you?

Do you befriend girls who are ignored by others because you value them as God's image-bearers? Or so they will vote for you for class president?

You get the idea. The difference between the true and the new is not simply a matter of actions; it is a matter of the heart. And here's the stickler—we usually do not know our own hearts. As Jeremiah 17:9 says, "The heart is deceitful above all things, and desperately sick; who can understand it?"

When helper actions flow from self-centered motives they are not true—they are hypocritical. They are polluted. Proverbs 27:19 tells us, "As in water face reflects face, so the heart of man reflects the man."

The girl who wants to become a true woman trusts God enough to ask Him to "Search me, O God, and know my heart! Try me and know my thoughts!" (Psalm 139:23).

She prays: "Create in me a clean heart, O God, and renew a right spirit within me" (Psalm 51:10).

And she prays for the life-giving grace of gratitude.

"I cry to you, O Lord; I say, 'You are my refuge, Attend to my cry . . . Deliver me . . . that I may give thanks to your name!'" (Psalm 142:5–7)

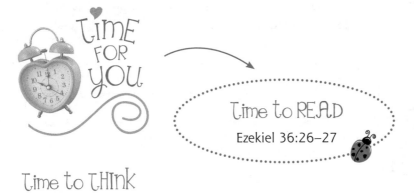

Time FOR you

Time to READ
Ezekiel 36:26–27

Time to THINK

What did you learn from this devotion?

What are your thoughts about Gratitude's Story?

_____

_____

_____

Time to PRAY

Select Scriptures in this devotion and write your prayer.

_____

_____

_____

_____

_____

_____

Time to LIVE FOR GOD'S GLORY

Gratitude is powerful because it turns us from self to God.
List several things about God for which you are grateful.

_____

_____

_____

_____

_____

Jillann's Story

Growing up in a family of five kids is chaotic, loud, and busy, but flesh and blood aren't what makes our family—its heart. My parents had three sons when they decided to adopt more children. The Lord led them to India, and to me, when I was 22 months old. When I was seven, we decided one more girl would make our family complete. Again the Lord led my parents to India and to my younger sister, Nance.

My wonderful family has shown me how important adoption is, and they've painted a picture of how Christ adopts us into His family. They have taught me that we adopt not because we are rescuers; we adopt because we are the rescued. A child does not initiate adoption; a parent chooses to adopt a child.

The Word teaches us we were once children of wrath (Ephesians 2:3), alienated from God (Colossians 1:21), and totally unable to save ourselves from our sin. The good news of the gospel is that God saw our need and reached down His hand of mercy to adopt me as His own.

The past nineteen years haven't been filled with just butterflies and rainbows. We are a normal family with issues any other family deals with, and I have the same struggles other teen girls experience—body image, doubting God's plan for my life, gossip, envy, going to youth group just to socialize, and the list goes on. The thing that keeps our family together is our understanding of Christ's sovereignty over all things and His perfect love for us.

One of my favorite quotes is from Francis Chan's book Crazy Love: "The irony is that while God doesn't need us but still wants us, we desperately need God but don't really want Him most of the time."

That is my struggle, and some days I just have to pray: Lord help me to want You.

The verse I try to remember in every circumstance is: "Fear not, for I have redeemed you; I have called you by name, you are mine" (Isaiah 43:1).

Words can't express how thankful I am to have grown up in a Christian home when I could still be in the caste system of Indian society. When I realize where I could have been and where God has brought me, the one word that comes to mind is "gratitude."

Jillann Starr, Jonesboro, Georgia

Gospel Power

Perhaps you are asking yourself questions I ask myself:

How can I live for God's glory rather than for myself?

How can I be a life-giver rather than a life-taker?

How can I help rather than hurt?

The answer is: We can't.

We live in a self-absorbed culture and we have self-absorbed hearts. *But* the gospel is powerful enough to save us from our sin and to liberate us from ourselves.

How powerful is it? The Bible calls it:

"The immeasurable greatness of his power toward us who believe, according to the working of his great might that he worked in Christ when he raised him from the dead . . . " (Ephesians 1:19–20).

Did you get that? If you have faith in Jesus, you have the same power in you that raised Him from the dead!

This power refers to the Holy Spirit.

"I will put my Spirit within you, and cause you to walk in my statutes and be careful to obey my rules . . . you shall be my people, and I will be your God" (Ezekiel 36:27–28).

> For I am not ashamed of the gospel, for it is the power of God for salvation to everyone who believes.
>
> ROMANS 1:16

This means that a Christian can never say, "I can't change . . . I can't stop . . . I can't forgive . . . I can't love."

By the power of His Spirit living in us, we can. The problem is we won't.

Living for God's glory begins in the heart as we repent of our sin and ask God to give us His power to change our attitudes and desires. This is the process of sanctification.

Sanctification is a slow process, but it is a good process. It is a life-giving process.

God created you to be a helper. Apart from Christ, doing this is impossible. With Christ it's possible, but it's still hard. It means dying to self—putting aside your own desires—and living for Christ. John the Baptist said it well: "He must increase, but I must decrease" (John 3:30).

Thankfully, Jesus gives us a Helper so we can be a helper. His promise in John 14:16–17 is electrifying: "And I will ask the Father, and he will give you another Helper, to be with you forever, even the Spirit of truth . . . he dwells with you and will be in you."

You can be a helper because, "God is our refuge and strength, a very present help in trouble" (Psalm 46:1).

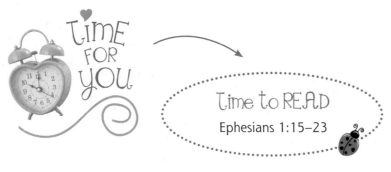

Time for you

Time to READ
Ephesians 1:15–23

Time to THINK

If you are a Christian, what are your thoughts about the power that is available to you?

What are your thoughts about Jillann's Story?

Time to PRAY

Are you willing to pray John 3:30? Use John 3:30 and Ephesians 1:15–23 to write your prayer.

Time to LIVE FOR GOD'S GLORY

Gratitude causes us to occupy less space in our heart and Jesus to occupy more space. What are some things about your life—your circumstances and abilities—for which you are grateful?

Aylin's Story

I grew up in a Christian home, and the Lord rescued me when I was very young, but for a long time I thought the gospel was relevant only to my salvation, not to the way I lived every day. Obviously with such a faulty focus I often had feelings of condemnation and guilt. Then our sovereign faithful One guided my steps, exposing me to people who love the gospel and are intentional in teaching from a gospel perspective. I began to understand the centrality of the gospel for all of life.

As I learned about the topic of womanhood through a gospel-centered perspective, I began to delight in God's design for me as a woman. The more I understood the gospel, the more I joyfully embraced my life-giver calling. Seeing biblical womanhood in the light of the story of redemption helped me to put so many other things in perspective. Now I understand that I have no power in me to live out my design, but that the gospel is the power I need.

It is exciting to trust the power of the gospel to transform me into a life-giver in all areas and roles of my life. May He increase, and may I decrease!

Aylin Michelen, Santo Domingo, Dominican Republic

(This story is adapted from TRUE, a discipleship curriculum for teen girls. Used by permission.)

13 Stiff-necked People

The young girl looked at me quizzically: "Okay, my purpose is to glorify God, but what that means is still sketchy to me."

You stiff-necked people . . . you always resist the Holy Spirit.

ACTS 7:51

Perhaps it is to you too. A fascinating story in Exodus 33–34 will help.

After Moses led God's people out of slavery in Egypt, he went up Mount Sinai and God gave him the Ten Commandments. While Moses was on the mountain, the Israelites did the unthinkable—they made and worshiped a golden calf.

God said to Moses: "Go up to a land flowing with milk and honey; but I will not go up among you, lest I consume you on the way, for you are a stiff-necked people" (Exodus 33:3).

They were stiff-necked—rebellious and stubborn—people, but they were God's people. They had whined and complained since they left Egypt. They had caused Moses much grief. If I had been in his place my decision would probably have been, "I'm not going with them either."

But Moses did an extraordinary thing. He prayed, for himself and for them. He asked God: "Please show me now your ways, that I may know you in order to find favor in your sight. Consider too that this nation is your people" (Exodus 33:13).

As we read about Moses, we can think of him as an illustration of Jesus, who continually prays for us, even when we are stiff-necked, because we are His people.

And God answered Moses' prayer. God told Moses: "My presence will go with you, and I will give you rest" (v. 14).

God's presence always gives rest to our souls. Moses needed the power of God's presence in order to live with stubborn people. But then Moses asked for something else: "Please show me your glory" (v. 18).

God had shown Moses the external brightness of His glory at the burning bush and at Mount Sinai (Exodus 3 and 19), but Moses needed to see the internal brightness of God's glory so he could show that glory to stiff-necked people. God said: "I will make all my goodness pass before you and will proclaim before you my name, 'The Lord' . . . But . . . you cannot see my face, for man shall not see me and live." And the Lord said, "Behold, there is a place by me where you shall stand on the rock, and while my glory passes by I will put you in a cleft of the rock, and I will cover you with my hand until I have passed by" (19–22).

God told moses to stand on the rock and He would put him in the rock.

While Moses stood on a physical rock, we are also to stand on a rock. And 1 Corinthians 10:4 tells us, the Rock is Jesus.

When, by God's grace, we are in Jesus, we can see what Moses saw and we can show it to others, even those who disappoint and hurt. What did Moses see? Read on . . .

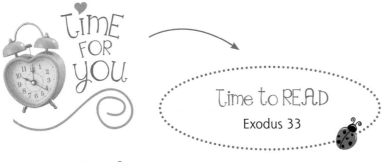

Time for you

Time to READ

Exodus 33

Time to THINK

When Moses asked to see God's glory, what did God say He would show him?

Where do we see the goodness of God's glory? See John 1:14 and Hebrews 1:1–3.

What are your thoughts about Aylin's Story?

Time to PRAY

Make Moses's prayer in Exodus 33:18 your prayer. Ask God to show you His glory, ask Him to show you Jesus, in His Word and to give you grace to reflect that goodness to others—even those who disappoint and hurt you.

Time to LIVE FOR GOD'S GLORY

List each member of your family, and beside the name write something about that person for which you are grateful. Then show your family the list.

Shining People

14

It was an audacious thing to ask, but I'm sure glad he asked it. When Moses asked to see God's glory, God said that He would show Moses His goodness. This is what we need to see in order to glorify God.

Moses said, "Please show me your glory."
EXODUS 33:18

"The LORD passed before him and proclaimed, 'The LORD, the LORD . . .'" (Exodus 34:6). Notice that in this scripture, "Lord" is in capital letters. This means it is the Hebrew word *Jehovah*. God's various names reveal different things about Him. Jehovah is His personal name. It shows us that He lives in personal relationship with His people, binds Himself to us in covenant loyalty, and promises to be our God.

Then God described His goodness: "A God merciful and gracious, slow to anger, and abounding in steadfast love and faithfulness, keeping steadfast love for thousands, forgiving iniquity and transgression and sin" (vv. 6–7).

Then He told Moses something extraordinary: "Behold, I am making a covenant. Before all your people I will do marvels, such as have not been created in all the earth or in any nation. And all the people among whom you are shall see the work of the Lord, for it is an awesome thing that I will do with you" (v. 10).

He did not say He would do an awesome thing *for* the Israelites, and in turn, us—though He surely does that—but *with* us.

What happened next is astonishing.

"When Moses came down from Mount Sinai . . . Moses did not know that the skin of his face shone because he had been talking with God" (v. 29). What blows my mind more than the fact that Moses's face was glowing from his time with God is that he was not aware of it! Moses was so bedazzled with God's glory that he forgot about himself. That's the way it works.

The more we are absorbed with self, the less we reflect God's glory.

The less we are absorbed with self, the more we reflect His glory.

let's recap:

- When we live in a personal relationship with the Lord through faith in Jesus, we see the glory of His goodness as we study His Word and know Him better.

- His goodness is His mercy, graciousness, slowness to anger, steadfast love, faithfulness, and forgiveness.

- God promises to do awesome things with us. And He does.

- He transforms stiff-necked people into shining people—people who are merciful, gracious, slow to anger, loving, faithful, and forgiving.

"And we all, with unveiled face, beholding the glory of the Lord, are being transformed into the same image from one degree of glory to another" (2 Corinthians 3:18).

Like Moses, we live in a sinful world and we live among sinful people. We can't change other people, and many times we cannot change our circumstances, but the gospel is powerful enough to change us. People and circumstances do not make us stiff-necked; our own sin does that. When we pray to see God's glory and to be transformed into His likeness, we begin to shine the light of His goodness to others.

The true woman is bedazzled by God's glory, and she is dazzling.

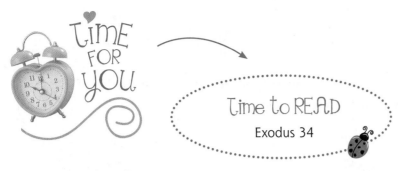

Time For You

Time to READ
Exodus 34

Time to THINK

- Are there stiff-necked people in your life?
- Are you stiff-necked or stubborn?
- What are your thoughts about being transformed from glory to greater glory? What will that look like in your life?

Time to PRAY

List the characteristics of God's goodness that are named in Exodus 34:6–7. Write your prayer asking God to transform your heart so you reflect these qualities.

Time to LIVE FOR GOD'S GLORY

What difference is practicing the grace of gratitude making in your attitudes and actions? Is it becoming easier for you to be grateful? Are you grumbling less? What are some ordinary, everyday things in your life for which you are grateful?

We Need Each Other

A young college woman was deeply troubled as she asked the following question: "How can I possibly think biblically about being a woman when I am constantly being told that independence is power, and that I should determine my own destiny and do what makes me happy?"

I understood her question. Your generation is growing up in a self-absorbed culture with the motto: "It's all about me." You are growing up in a culture that says the only difference between males and females is biological.

This was my answer to that young woman: "Go to some women in your church and ask them to speak the truth about womanhood into your life. Ask them to disciple you. Ask them to show and tell you what God says about being a woman."

This answer was not my idea. It is God's plan.

"We will . . . tell to the coming generation the glorious deeds of the Lord . . . which he commanded our fathers to teach to their children, that the next generation might know them, the children yet unborn, and arise and tell them to their children, so that they should set their hope in God and not forget the works of God" (Psalm 78:4–7).

Titus 2:3–5 also tells us that older women are to train the young women.

One of the glorious deeds of God that older women are to tell the next generation is that God created them in His image, male and female He created them. Older women are to train younger women to live for God's glory as a woman. This training is not simply teaching a lesson; older women are to share their lives with younger women. We are to learn about womanhood in the context of loving relationships. Paul describes this kind of discipleship in 1 Thessalonians 2:7–8: "We were gentle among you, like a nursing mother taking care of her own children. So, being affectionately desirous of you, we were ready to share with you not only the gospel of God but also our own selves, because you had become very dear to us."

This means that younger women—*you*—should seek out older women and learn from them. This may be your mother or grandmother, your youth leader, a high school or college girl who is only a few years older than you, or any women who love Jesus and live for His glory.

And think about this—you are an "older woman" to younger girls.

Being a Christian is not a solo journey. God intends for one generation to help and encourage the next generation to live for His glory. A wise girl will recognize her need for older women in her life and she will ask them to help her become a true woman.

Q. **Why should we unselfishly share our lives with others?**

A: So that "the word of God may not be reviled" (Titus 2:5). Our magnificent mission is so much bigger than ourselves. Our purpose is to honor and glorify the King of kings.

Time For You

Time to READ
Psalm 78:1–8

Time to THINK

Think about women who are influencing you to live for God's glory. Name one of them and list some things you see in her life that you would like to learn and to apply in your own life.

Time to PRAY

Use Psalm 78 and Titus 2:3–5 to write a prayer thanking God for the older women in your life.

Time to LIVE FOR GOD'S GLORY

What are some ways you are thankful for the woman you named above? Show her your list, and ask her to help you live for God's glory. Ask her to help you develop the holy habit of gratitude.

Anna Kate's Story

Anna Kate was eight years old when her grandmother died. She wrote this and read it at her grandmother's funeral:

Nana was a courageous person. I will never know how she always had a smile on her face, but I do know how she lived. She lived a great life through Jesus Christ alone. And I know that she made every minute of her life good by supporting her friends and family, daughter, son, granddaughter, grandson, nieces, nephews, and especially her husband, my Papa.

It is hard for all of us to see her go, but she is walking streets of gold and touching fences of pearls. We all know she is in a better place.

She was cool, courageous, nice, loving, encouraging, fun, and funny. She was my best friend. Some people don't even get to have grandparents because they die too soon. I am blessed I even had her for eight years.

I believe she was suffering more than any of us knew. Even on days she was not feeling well, she still said, "I am doing fine."

She is truly my hero. She still means the world to me. I am amazed by the legacy she left. Everybody would pray for her. We prayed for her at school. At church we prayed for her, but we have no reason to be mad at God. He did best. We all know she was in pain, but now she has a perfect body in heaven.

If I hadn't known her for these eight years, I wouldn't even be close to being the girl I am today.

Anna Kate Cartwright, Douglasville, Georgia

(This story is adapted from TRUE, a discipleship curriculum for teen girls. Used by permission.)

16 The Promise Is Kept

Mary was probably a teenager —maybe your age—when she heard the news straight from the angel's mouth: "Greetings, O favored one, the Lord is with you!" (Luke 1:28).

> Her offspring . . . shall bruise your head.
>
> GENESIS 3:15

"Favored one" means that she had received God's grace. He chose her because of His grace, not because she was better than others. Then came the angelic announcement that she would be the mother of the Offspring God had promised in Genesis 3:15.

"And behold, you will conceive in your womb and bear a son, and you shall call his name Jesus . . . and of his kingdom there will be no end" (Luke 1:31, 33).

It is remarkable that Mary maintained her composure enough to ask an intelligent question—but grace produces maturity: "How will this be, since I am a virgin?" (v.34).

The angel answered: "The Holy Spirit will come upon you, and the power of the Most High will overshadow you; therefore the child to be born will be called holy—the Son of God" (v.35).

God would step into human history as a man to do what Adam failed to do—live a life of perfect obedience so He could be the sacrifice for the sin of His people.

Mary's answer to this good news is the response of a true woman:

"Behold, I am the servant of the Lord . . . "

i.e.—Her purpose was God's glory.

"Let it be to me according to your word" (v. 38).

i.e.,—Her authority was God's Word.

. . . .

The angel left, and so did Mary. Luke tells us that "Mary . . . went with haste . . . to a town in Judah, and she entered the house of Zechariah and greeted Elizabeth" (Luke 1:39–40).

As soon as Elizabeth saw Mary she said: "Blessed are you among women . . . blessed is she who believed . . . what was spoken to her from the Lord" (Luke 1:44, 45).

Elizabeth welcomed, encouraged, and instructed Mary. And Mary sang a song of gratitude that has blessed God's church through the ages: "My soul magnifies the Lord, and my spirit rejoices in God my Savior . . ." (Luke 1:46–47).

Like Mary, when you ask godly women to help you become a true woman, your life will become a song of gratitude to God our Savior.

Eventually Mary left Elizabeth's home. She gave birth to Jesus, and she watched Him grow up.

In John 2 we read that one day Mary and Jesus were at a wedding together. The host ran out of wine, and Mary told Jesus about this problem. Then she turned to the servants and said, "Do whatever he tells you" (John 2:5).

They did, and Jesus changed water to wine.

When we do what Jesus tells us to do, we will be changed from life-takers to life-givers.

Jesus said: "If you love me, you will keep my commandments" (John 14:15).

Time to READ

Luke 1:26–56

Time to THINK

What do you think of Mary's definition of herself as the servant of the Lord and her strong declaration that His Word was her authority? Is this your definition and declaration?

What are your thoughts about Anna Kate's Story?

Time to PRAY

Use Mary's definition and declaration, and her prayer (Luke 1:46–55) to write your prayer of gratitude for God's grace in your life.

_____

_____

_____

_____

_____

_____

Time to LIVE FOR GOD'S GLORY

What difference does our definition of ourselves and our declaration of our authority make in our lives? What difference does it make in your life? List two or three specific ways God's grace has transformed you, and thank Him.

_____

_____

_____

_____

_____

_____

_____

_____

Another Mary's Story

When I was ten, my dad was my best friend. If I had a problem or needed guidance, he was always there to help. But then the unimaginable happened. Dad had a massive heart attack. In an instant, he was gone, and I knew I would never get him back.

I was angry with God for taking my father away, and I took it out on everyone. I tried to replace God in my life with anything I could find: academics, sports, leadership positions, awards, and friends.

Yet through my Christian school and church, God continually reminded me that He is a Father to the fatherless and our help in time of need. Each time I went to a chapel service at school or a weekend retreat with my youth group, the message seemed to be the same: God is always there, always ready to love us.

My hard heart slowly melted.

I surrendered my life to Christ again and realized that I needed to embrace His plan for my life rather than trying to piece together a plan of my own.

Nearly ten years have passed since my dad's death, and now I see the situation more clearly. I see that Christ was glorified and that my personal relationship with Him was solidified during those years.

And through it all my mom was a wonderful example of biblical womanhood. By God's grace she kept going when I thought God had abandoned us, and she kept her patience with me during my years of struggle. She knew God would never leave us, even as my own faith faltered. Her relationship with Him is her strength, and He has never failed her. Now I know that He will never fail me either.

—Mary Kuipers, Acworth, Georgia

(This story is from TRUE, a discipleship curriculum for teen girls. Used by permission.)

Becoming a True Woman

17

hat a fascinating verse. When you think of women as pillars, what is the first image that comes to your mind? For me it's a woman who was literally changed into a pillar: Lot's wife. The story is told in Genesis 19:1–26.

Lot was sitting at the gate of the city one night when two angels came to visit. Lot greeted them and offered them hospitality, then the angels told Lot the reason for their visit: "'We are about to destroy this place, because the outcry against its people has become great before the LORD, and the LORD has sent us to destroy it' . . . As morning dawned, the angels urged Lot, saying, 'Up! Take your wife and your two daughters who are here, lest you be swept away in the punishment of the city . . . Escape for your life. Do not look back'. . . But Lot's wife, behind him, looked back, and she became a pillar of salt" (Genesis 19:13, 15, 17, 26).

The Hebrew word translated "pillar" in Genesis 19 is not the same word that is used in Psalm 144. The word in Genesis 19 means to be stopped and trapped in a still, upright position.

Consider Jesus' warning: "Just as it was in the days of Lot—they were eating and drinking, buying and selling, planting and building, but on the day when Lot went out from Sodom, fire and sulfur rained from heaven and destroyed them all—so will it be on the day when the Son of Man is revealed . . . Remember Lot's wife. Whoever seeks to preserve his life will lose it, but whoever loses his life will keep it" (Luke 17:28–33).

The girl or woman who seeks to preserve her life—who lives for herself—is trapped in immature self-centeredness. Her purpose is personal happiness, and her authority is herself, so she is a life-taker in her relationships. Living for self is ultimately self-destructive.

The word translated "pillar" in Psalm 144 refers to a functional, supportive, often beautifully carved pillar. In ancient times these pillars were frequently carved in the shape of beautiful women. This kind of pillar gives support, stability, and beauty to a building.

Carving is tedious. It is a slow and sometimes painful process to be carved, but our loving, sovereign Sculptor uses every painful relationship and circumstance in our lives to slowly chip away at our self-sufficiency and selfishness.

Carving is a tender process. Our Father's gentle hand lovingly holds us even as He scrapes the rough places in our hearts to make them smooth.

Carving transforms. As we trust our Father and ask Him for grace to submit to His authority and live for His glory, our character is slowly and surely shaped into His image. We become like Him. He transforms us into true women who lose our lives so that we may be filled with the life of Christ.

The Lord God carves each of His daughters into a pillar who gives gospel beauty and stability to her relationships and situations—and a true woman emerges.

Nineteenth century pastor John Angell James, in his book *Female Piety*, wrote:

A community is not likely to be overthrown where woman fulfills her mission; for by the power of her noble heart over the hearts of others, she will raise it from its ruins, and restore it again to prosperity and joy.

Are you ready to be carved? In the next section Mary Kassian will help you think through what it means to be a life-giver in very practical ways. She will challenge you to be wise and not wild. I pray that the Holy Spirit will give you grace to submit to God's tender carving—though at times it may be tedious—and that you will be transformed by the power of the gospel into a true woman who reflects God's glory.

Time for you

Time to READ

Proverbs 9

Time to THINK

The word for pillar in Proverbs 9:1 is the same as the word in Psalm 144:12. What contrast do you see in Proverbs 9 between wisdom and folly? Where does the way of wisdom lead (vv. 6, 10–11)? Where does the way of folly lead (v. 18)?

What are your thoughts about Mary's Story?

Time to PRAY

Use Psalm 144:12 and Proverbs 9:10 to write your prayer.

Time to LIVE FOR GOD'S GLORY

What has been most helpful to you in these devotions? What are two or three things that you plan to do to become a true woman? Share your plan with an older woman and ask her to help you.

mary Kate's Story

When our granddaughter Mary Kate was sixteen, my husband and I took her to Washington, D.C. When we toured the United States Capitol building, we marveled at the magnificent Rotunda with its 180-feet high dome. Then the guide took us to the lower level and we saw the original meeting place of the Supreme Court. But what fascinated us most was a large star on the floor.

The guide explained that the star is the center of the Capitol building and of the city of Washington. All the streets in Washington are laid out and numbered from this point. This star is directly under the soaring dome we had seen earlier.

We formed a line and each person put his or her foot on the star. After our turn I took Mary Kate's hand and pulled her back for a bigger view. "What do you see?" I asked.

We looked at forty massive columns—pillars—that surrounded the star and supported the floor of the Rotunda. Mary Kate grinned and said, "Our daughters will be like pillars carved to adorn a palace."

Overwhelmed with gratitude I said, "Mary Kate, don't ever forget this. If we had not come to this lower level we would not have seen these pillars, but if they ever begin to weaken, that marvelous dome is in danger of collapsing. If Christian women forsake our creation design and redemptive calling, our homes, churches, and culture will begin to crumble. But by God's grace a few strong pillars can provide support and stability. You are becoming what you will be. Will you be a pillar of salt or a pillar of grace?"

Letter from Mary

Hey Girls!

I hope you enjoyed learning about the foundations of true womanhood in the first section of this book. I'm so proud of you for putting in the effort to get this far!

Susan showed us that womanhood is part of the amazing plan God had in mind before the foundation of the world. She had you spend time in Genesis, looking at how and why God created male and female. She showed you that becoming a true woman is all about living for God's glory.

And that's not an abstract idea.

- It's more relevant than the astrophysics, quasars, and black holes discussed in your science text.

- It's more significant than your language teacher's instruction on how to conjugate a verb.

- It's more pertinent than the philosophies and theories of world politicians.

Living for God's glory isn't just a concept or theory. It's a practical way of life and affects the choices you make every day.

The choices you make at this stage in your life are so critical.

Over the next few years you'll make the transition from being a child to being an adult. You'll leave girlhood behind. You'll become a woman. That means you'll have to deal with male-female relationships from an entirely different angle than when you were a kid. Over the next few years, you'll be making choices about

- What it means to be a woman,

- How you'll interact with men,

- Your wardrobe and appearance,

- Your ideas about romance,

- Your approach to dating,

- Your physical and sexual conduct,

- The boundaries you'll observe,

- Your perspective on marriage,

- Your schedule and habits,

- Your goals and priorities,

- . . . and a lot of other things.

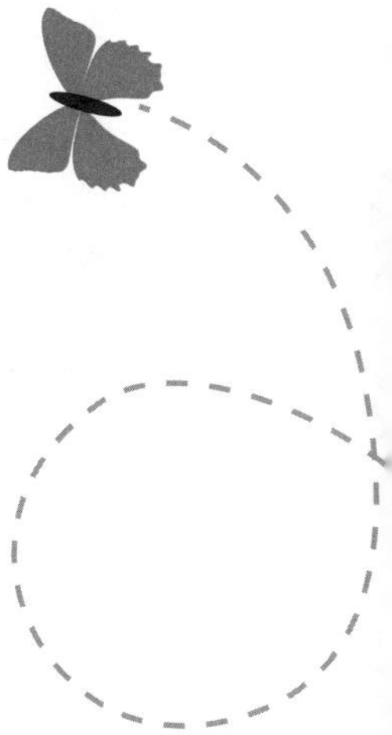

If you want to be a true woman, you'll need to make wise, godly choices!

Many girls don't. They just don't take the time think about it. They're naive. Unprepared. They don't understand the difference between the way the world works and God's way. Sadly, they end up making bad choices and messing up their lives.

The Bible urges us to be careful and intentional about the way we live: "Do not walk as unwise [wild] but as wise!" (see Ephesians 5:15)

In the second part of this *Becoming God's True Woman* devotional, I'm going to show you some ways you can be a woman who lives for God's glory. We'll spend time in Proverbs—the Bible's book of wisdom—figuring out what it means, practically, for a girl to walk as wise and not wild.

A wise king wrote the book of Proverbs for his sons. Among other things, the father teaches the young princes how to tell the difference between girls who are Wild Things (life-takers) and those who are Wise Things (life-givers). In one chapter (the famous Proverbs 31) the queen offers her perspective too.

The parents wanted their sons to associate with the right kind of women and avoid the wrong kind. They knew that the future and success of their boys' lives depended on the sort of women they were around.

I know how they must have felt! My husband and I have raised three sons. We've had the same concerns. We know girls have the power to be life-givers or life-takers. We've worried when our sons have made poor choices about women, and we've rejoiced when they've made wise choices.

One of the greatest joys and blessings of our lives has been seeing our oldest son marry a life-giver—a young woman we adore, who is truly a wise woman of God. We're praying that our other two sons will experience the same blessing!

By studying Proverbs, you'll learn a lot about how to *be* the right kind of woman. You'll learn the difference between wise and wild. You'll learn about which attitudes and behaviors to adopt and which to avoid. You'll learn about girls, guys, friends, relationships, responsibility, and making good decisions. You'll learn how to live as God's true woman!

Becoming a true woman is all about living for God's glory—and that's not an abstract idea. It's practical. It affects the choices you make every day.

Scattered throughout Part 2 are pages where you'll "Get It from the Girls." These pages contain notes and comments written by teen girls in response to questions I posted on my blog (www.girlsgonewise.com). I'm so glad they took the time to share their thoughts. I found their input insightful and helpful—and I think you will too.

The world feeds us a lot of false messages. Taking the time to discover what the Bible says about true womanhood now (while you still have a curfew) will help you make wise choices for your future, and help you avoid the pain and heartache that results from going down the wrong path.

You can complete the lessons in this section at your own pace, but please be diligent and faithful to do them. They'll help you enormously as you make the transition into womanhood. I promise they will!

As the wise king noted,

"Blessed is the one who finds wisdom, and the one who gets understanding!" (Proverbs 3:13).

So you go, girl! Keep at it!

I'm cheering for you!

With affection,

Mary

Wise Up!

18

Proverbs talks about two types of girls: those who are wild, and those who are wise. I think girls genuinely want to make smart choices. But sadly, most don't have a clue how to go about doing that.

When I was shooting a video for my book *Girls Gone Wise*, I took my film crew to a college campus and asked female students the question, "How would you define wisdom?"

> Blessed is the one who finds wisdom, and the one who gets understanding, for the gain from her is better than gain from silver and her profit better than gold. She is more precious than jewels, and nothing you desire can compare with her.
>
> PROVERBS 3:13–15

One girl defined it as book smarts combined with street smarts. Another said it was the know-how and experience you gain in college. But can you guess what the most popular answer was?

It was, "Umm . . . I don't know!"

Not only did those college students have trouble telling me what wisdom was, they also had trouble telling me where a girl could find it. Most supposed that the best source of wisdom would be a parent, teacher, or friend.

Parents are undoubtedly a good source of guidance, but the Bible has a different answer about what wisdom is and where to find it. Look at what these verses say about wisdom:

"In [Jesus Christ] are hidden all the treasures of wisdom and knowledge" (Colossians 2:3).

"For the Lord gives wisdom; from his mouth come knowledge and understanding" (Proverbs 2:6).

"The fear of the Lord is the beginning of wisdom; all those who practice it have a good understanding" (Psalm 111:10).

A girl who has committed herself to a relationship with Jesus Christ is a Wise Thing, not a Wild Thing. God's glory is her purpose and His Word is her authority for how she should conduct herself in every area of life, including her relationships with guys. She "fears" the Lord. That doesn't mean she's scared of Him. It simply means that she respects and obeys what He has to say. She upholds His Word as her authority.

Wild is the opposite of wise. Wild is another word for what the Bible calls foolish, wayward, evil, ignorant, or unwise. Wild is what we are whenever we disregard God and rely instead on the world's advice or on what seems right in our own eyes.

The Lord says:

....

"Whoever trusts in his own mind is a fool, but he who walks in wisdom will be delivered" (Proverbs 28:26).

"The discerning sets his face toward wisdom, but the eyes of a fool are on the ends of the earth" (Proverbs 17:24).

A Wise Thing lives God's way. She sets her face toward His wisdom. A Wild Thing does life her own way. Her eyes are "on the ends of the earth." In other words, she looks everywhere except to the Lord for advice.

Do you know who the first Wild Thing was? It was Eve. She went wild when she listened to the serpent and relied on her own smarts instead of trusting God's wisdom.

Satan's strategy hasn't changed. He still tries to mess girls up by getting them to look to the world, rely on their own intelligence, and disregard God's insight about the way they should live.

A Wild Thing relies on her own "smarts," but a Wise Thing looks to the Lord for direction.

I pray that you won't fall for that deceptive trap. Be wise and not wild! Learn what the Lord says about true womanhood and choose to live His way.

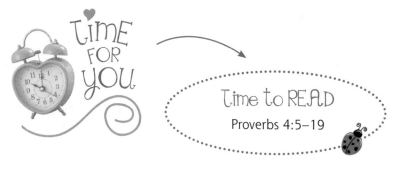

Time FOR You

Time to READ
Proverbs 4:5–19

Time to THINK

Using Proverbs 4:5–19, make a list of all the benefits of following the way of wisdom.

Time to PRAY

Write out a prayer based on Proverbs 3:13–15. Ask the Lord to help you value wisdom above everything else you might desire.

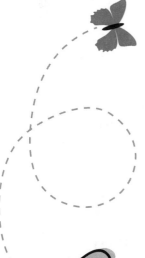

Time to LIVE FOR GOD'S GLORY

Look around your room at all the things you value—like a jewelry box, a favorite book, your cell phone, awards, or mementos of special occasions. Ask yourself, "Do I value wisdom more than this?"

As you go through your day, make a habit of asking yourself if you value wisdom more than other things—more than popularity, fitting in, having a boyfriend, watching a particular movie, or listening to a particular song, for example.

Ask the Lord to help you desire wisdom more.

19 Deadened by the Drip

Advertisers rely on a powerful technique called "drip marketing" to get you to buy their products. They know that "dripping" their message slowly and steadily in small bits over an extended period of time (like water dripping from a tap), is much more effective than quickly pouring the message out.

> Blessed is the man who walks not in the counsel of the wicked, nor stands in the way of sinners, nor sits in the seat of scoffers; but his delight is in the law of the Lord, and on his law he meditates day and night.
>
> PSALM 1:1–2

Research shows that when people have heard a message about thirty times, it "takes hold" in their sub-consciousness. As the message is repeatedly dripped into a person's mind, it sticks, and the person is much more likely to buy-in to that particular product or idea.

Drip marketing is based on this simple fact: Steady, repeated exposure to an idea typically results in a person accepting that idea.

Why is this important for you to know? Because the world constantly "drips" messages about womanhood into your mind.

So, for example, if you hear the song message, "I kissed a girl and I liked it!" often enough, you'll start to think that it's perfectly normal and acceptable for girls to kiss girls and enjoy it. And you might start to wonder if you should try it.

The drip marketing of that message will influence you to buy in to that false idea. Without your realizing it, it will subtly affect your beliefs. And especially if you fail to intentionally counter that lie with God's truth.

That was the downfall of the Wild Thing in Proverbs. The writer explains: "Her feet go down to death; her steps follow the path to Sheol; she does not ponder the path of life; her ways wander, and she does not know it" (Proverbs 5:5–6).

The mistake of a Wild Thing is that she doesn't intentionally think about how to live a godly life. She goes about her daily business and neglects to ponder the way of the Lord.

It's not that she willfully snubs God. She just doesn't take the time or make the effort to figure out what His path is or how to walk in it.

Instead, the drip marketing of the world gets into her system and numbs her sensibilities. Her constant exposure to mass media poisons the way she thinks and behaves. She doesn't even realize that she's wandering down the wrong path!

Did you know that according to the U.S. Census Bureau, the average girl exposes herself to 3,596 hours of popular media each year?

For hours and hours each day, the world's perspectives about beauty, sex, relationships, appearance, money, possessions, power, prestige, self-indulgence, and personal rights drip into her system.

Constantly listening to these messages inevitably affects your thinking. It's like a drip, drip, drip, drip quietly pounding on your head and your heart.

Are you being deadened by the drip?

If you are wise, you will make sure your thoughts about womanhood are shaped by the Word instead of the drip marketing of the world. You'll be careful to tune out the message of the world and tune in to the ways of the Lord instead.

FACT: If you take in an "average" amount of TV and other popular media, by the time you are 65, the accumulated "drip" will add up to 40 solid years! Wow! That's a whole lot of worldly counsel! Do you need to reduce your daily media intake?

TiME FOR YOU

Time to READ

Philippians 4:8 and
Romans 12:2

Time to THINK

Think about the messages you are exposing yourself to—on TV, in movies, magazines, books, the Internet, and music. How well does your media consumption follow the guidelines of Philippians 4:8?

Do you need to make any adjustments?

Time to PRAY

Pray a prayer based on Psalm 1:1–2. Ask the Lord to help you avoid walking in the counsel of the ungodly and have the courage and strength to walk His way instead.

Time to LIVE FOR GOD'S GLORY

Don't kid yourself. You *will* be affected by the messages you expose yourself to! So it's important to minimize your exposure to messages that conflict with God's Word. That may mean making some tough decisions about turning off a particular TV show, not going to see a particular movie, or not reading a certain magazine or book.

Ask yourself yesterday's question: "Do I value this entertainment more than I value wisdom?"

Evaluate whether the content passes the Philippians 4:8 test. If it doesn't, make the wise choice. Turn it off or walk away.

What you spend your time with and allow your mind to dwell on will be displayed in your life. Girls need to realize that they should only spend their time enjoying the words, sounds, and images they want to become.—Allison, age 17

Girls are often influenced by media in very subconscious ways. If Hollywood presents a certain activity or item as being the "in thing," then the girls will often feel they need to behave that way or have that thing, because they feel that their worth is attached to the way others perceive them.—Jacqueline, age 17

Many girls watch or listen to things that they know are wrong just because it's popular and everyone is doing it. The problem is that then they become immune or okay with evil and just ignore it. They become desensitized. But Romans 12 says we should hate evil and cling to what is good. God doesn't want us to feel comfortable with sin.—Jenna, age 14

Popular media will hurt us. As we watch and listen to culture's ideals, our hearts and attitudes will slowly morph. We must learn how to apply a biblical worldview to what we are seeing. It's a choice and it does matter.—RuthAnne, age 17

If someone walked into the room would you want them looking at that show? Or dwelling on that book? If the answer is no, shut it off, close it, or throw it out.—Morgan, age 16

*Tape a Scripture verse about keeping your heart or eyes pure to your computer or TV screen. Turn off things that don't line up with Scripture. It's that simple.
—Clarie, age 18*

*I use Philippians 4:8 as my guide! If the media is not leading me to be more holy and Christlike and makes me long for the world, then it most likely isn't what I need to be watching or listening to! "Does it honor Christ?" That's the big question.
—RuthAnne, age 17*

Try to ask yourself if this is something that Christ would want you to watch/listen to. Also, ask yourself, If this was happening in real life in front of me would I be watching it?—Jenna, age 14

Consider whether you would be ashamed of your media choices if you were hanging out with Jesus—because you are, every single minute of every single day.—Allison, age 17

20

Dress to Impress

In Proverbs chapter 7, the wise king tells his son a story about a typical Wild Thing. In a nutshell, the story is about how she seduces a naïve young man. The father mentions several characteristics that are typical of a life-taker. Can you guess which characteristic he mentions first?

> Rather, clothe yourselves with the Lord Jesus Christ, and do not think about how to gratify the desires of the sinful nature.
>
> ROMANS 13:14, NIV1984

If you took a hint from the title of today's devotion and guessed, "The way she dresses," you'd be right!

"And behold, the woman meets him, dressed as a prostitute" (Proverbs 7:10).

One of the telltale marks of a Wild Thing is that she dresses "as a prostitute." The girl wasn't actually a prostitute. She was a respectable, married, church-going, young woman. But like a prostitute, she dressed with the intent of enticing and arousing the sexual attention of guys. Her aim was to look "hot" and "sexy" in their eyes.

Every girl wants to look and feel attractive. And there's nothing wrong with that. That's a natural, God-given desire.

But here's the difference between a wild and wise perspective on looks:

A Wild Thing's main concern is what people think about her looks, but a Wise Thing's main concern is what God thinks about her looks.

According to the Bible, the clothes we wear are an outward, visible symbol of an inward, spiritual reality. Read that statement again. It's important!

Think about the very first time in history people started wearing clothes. Do you know what their clothes looked like, and where and why they were made?

- Here's a hint: They were green.

- Here's another hint: They weren't made of cloth.

- Here's a final hint: They were made in the garden of Eden.

After they sinned, Adam and Eve twisted leafy coverings together in a feeble attempt to hide their nakedness and make themselves presentable to God.

But it didn't work. The fig leaves were inadequate.

Despite their best efforts, they couldn't make themselves presentable. Sin made that impossible. So God did what they were unable to do. He shed the blood of a lamb and clothed them. By means of a bloody sacrifice, God covered their sin and shame and made them presentable (Genesis 3:21).

God was actually the first fashion designer! The clothing He made pointed to the time when He would sacrifice His Son, Jesus, to pay the penalty for our sin and clothe us in the righteousness of Christ. Jesus covers our sin and makes us presentable. The reason we wear clothes is to bear witness to this amazing spiritual truth.

Later we'll talk about what that means for your wardrobe. But for now, I just want you to realize that if you dress to impress people (yourself included) then you're missing the point of what clothes are all about.

God gave us clothes as a physical reminder that spiritually, we need to dress in the right way.

Fig leaves are between 10 to 12 inches long and palm-shaped, with three to seven lobes. They have a rough top and a hairy underside. Adam and Eve would have twisted or hooked the leaves together in an attempt to cover themselves up. Can you imagine how relieved they must have felt when God replaced those stiff, itchy, ridiculous-looking fig leaves with soft, durable lambskin garments?

TimE FOR YOU

TimE to READ

Galatians 3:27 ▪ Colossians 3:10–14
▪ Revelation 3:18

TimE to THINK

According to these verses, what "garments" does the Lord
want you to clothe yourself in?

Why does He want you to wear these?

Can you think of a situation where "putting on Christ" would make
your behavior look different than someone who doesn't wear Jesus?

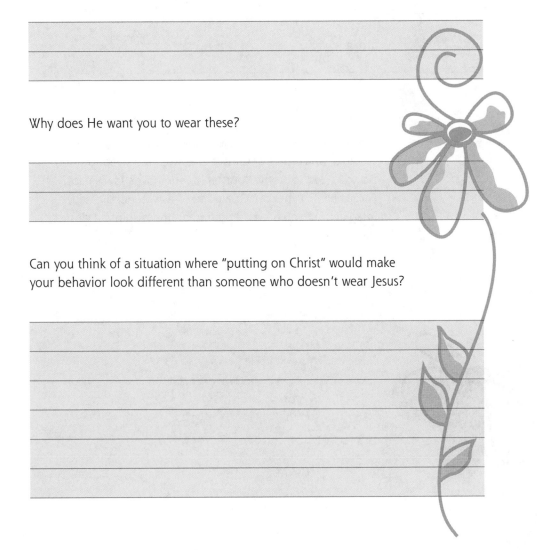

Time to PRAY

Use Romans 13:14 to write a prayer. Ask the Lord to help you be more concerned about how you're dressed spiritually than how you're dressed physically. Thank Him for His covering.

Time to LIVE FOR GOD'S GLORY

The next time you pick some clothes out of your closet, consider which part of Christ's character you need to put on. Do you need to clothe yourself in more love? Joy? Peace? Forgiveness? Patience? Or kindness? As you get dressed, imagine that you are also putting on those spiritual clothes.

I think every single girl on Earth has struggled with appearance.—Dania, age 16

I have struggled with thinking I'm not pretty, I need to lose weight, my hair isn't perfect, my clothes aren't cool enough . . . But every morning I look into the mirror and say that though I'm not the prettiest girl in the world, I'm beautiful to God and that's all that matters. And that truly is all that matters!—Emily, age 16

It's not the outside that counts; it's the inside. As long as you shine on the inside the outside will shine too.—Chevonne, age 13

If you're worried about what you look like, think of this. Jesus has said to us, "You are beautiful; beloved; you are mine. You are my bride." What is more beautiful than a bride on her wedding day? And we get to live EVERY SINGLE DAY as the bride of Christ. NEVER doubt that you are amazing, wonderful, and beautiful.—Montana, age 18

There have always been little things about my body I have struggled to accept—my toes were too long and bony, my eyebrows too bushy, my hair too thin. God has been teaching me that I am being discontent and ungrateful when I choose to dwell on my "imperfections." He has created me the way He did with a specific plan in mind. I've been learning to be content with the way He's made me and rejoice, knowing His plan for me is bigger than the way my nose looks.—Allison, age 17

The Lord didn't want His people to obsess about the appearance of the temple and forget about who lived inside. Our body is the temple of the Holy Spirit. Our appearance should let God's glory shine. It would be horrible if someone missed seeing Jesus in us because of our over-the-top clothing, or thickly painted face, or anything like that.—Claire, age 18

A girl is beautiful to God if she has a godly heart. Really, if our hearts aren't being sanctified by Christ, no matter how much makeup we put on we are still ugly and dirty. When we give all to Christ and surrender our looks and lives, He begins to change our views on ourselves and on the true meaning of beauty.—RuthAnne, age 17

What Not to Wear

21

Of all God's creatures, only humans wear clothing. We didn't at first. Adam and Eve didn't start the trend because they wanted to look fashionable or keep warm. The main reason people feel compelled to cover their nakedness is due to our fallen condition. Ever since the tragic day sin entered the world, we've felt the need to cover up.

> Likewise also that women should adorn themselves in respectable [becoming] apparel, with modesty [decency] and self-control [moderation].
>
> 1 TIMOTHY 2:9

Clothes are an object lesson.

- They bear witness to the fact that we've lost the glory and beauty of our original sin-free selves.

- They confess that we need God's covering to atone for our sin and get rid of our shame.

- They testify to the fact that that God solved the problem of sin with the blood of His own Son.

- They remind us daily that we need to clothe ourselves in the righteousness of Christ.

- They direct our attention forward to the time when we will be "further clothed" with white, imperishable garments (2 Corinthians 5:4 NKJV, Revelation 3:5).

As I said before: The clothes we wear are an outward, visible symbol of an inward, spiritual reality.

And that has implications for the way you dress.

First, it means that what you look like spiritually is far more important than what you look like physically. A Wise Thing commits far more time and energy to dressing herself up on the inside than on the outside.

Second, although external appearance is not the most important, it's not totally unimportant either. The visible should point to the invisible. The symbol should point to the reality.

In the end, your clothes aren't meant to be about you—they're meant to display deep spiritual truths about the beauty of the gospel.

So how do you decide what and what not to wear? Here are three questions that will help you decide:

1. Is it becoming?

A lot of instruction is packed into 1 Timothy 2:9. To begin, it says your clothes should be "respectable." In other words; they should suit, flatter, fit, or "become" who you are as a child of God. Not only that, they should suit your body type, your femininity, the other clothes you'll wear, and the occasion and place you intend to wear them. This word indicates that your appearance should be put together nicely—inside and out.

2. Is it decent?

Dressing decently means you agree with the Lord about the real purpose of clothing. It means that your clothes tell the truth about the gospel by covering your "nakedness" as adequately as the clothing of Christ covers your sin. This means that you choose clothes that are modest, and not provocative or seductive or that draw attention to your private parts. You cover up out of respect for the Lord, the gospel, your Christian brothers, and yourself. Christ has made you spiritually decent; therefore you should dress in a physically decent way.

3. Is it moderate?

Clothing should also be moderate—reasonable and not crazy. We're supposed to govern our wardrobe choices with a sense of temperance, simplicity, and self-control. The word in this verse implies that we should avoid crazy extremes in fashion, spending crazy amounts of money, and stuffing our closets crazy-full of clothes.

Times and fashions change. The Bible doesn't give us a detailed list of rules about clothes. But understanding the purpose of clothing, asking yourself these three questions, and relying on the guidance of the Holy Spirit will help you practically figure out what and what not to wear.

TiME FOR YOU

Time to READ
1 Peter 3:3–5

Time to THINK

In your own words, explain why God created clothing.

_____

_____

_____

_____

How does God's perspective on beauty and clothing differ from the world's perspective?

_____

_____

_____

_____

What clothing "wows" God the most?

_____

_____

_____

_____

Time to PRAY

Use 1 Timothy 2:9 to write out a prayer, asking the Lord to help you dress in the right way.

Time to LIVE FOR GOD'S GLORY

Write out 1 Timothy 2:9 and the corresponding three questions (on page 99) on a recipe card or small piece of paper. Tape them to your mirror.

Each day when you get dressed, read the verse and consider the questions. Ask the Lord to help you decide what and what not to wear.

You may want to keep another copy in your purse or wallet to consult when you're shopping or trying on outfits in dressing rooms.

Get It from the Girls . . .

Modest (mod-ist) *Held back by a sense of what is fit and proper; not brash or forward; having or showing a decency of thought and behavior; humble; holding back from calling attention to oneself.*

If a girl is modest she won't reveal personal parts of her body that are meant to be hidden.—Elisha, age 13

Modesty to me is beauty. It outwardly symbolizes what Christ has done to our hearts —made them new, clean, and worthy of coming into God's presence . . . that's what modesty is about.—RuthAnne, age 17

Modesty means guarding what is private and behaving in a way of respect so as not to defraud men. I've struggled with wanting to push the boundary line when it comes to modesty. I wish I could show just a little cleavage or wear a swim suit so I can show just a peek of those abs I've been working out at the gym to get. However, during those times of longing I remind myself of the special privilege of saving these things for my future husband's enjoyment.—Allison, age 17

Although some styles of clothing are definitely immodest, I think modesty has more to do with a mindset than anything else. Even jeans and a T-shirt can be worn with the wrong intentions.—Montana, age 18

To be modest, you first have to know why you are being modest. I think that a lot of girls are only wearing modest clothes because their parents make them or their church tells them to.—Hannah, age 20

I used to think modesty was boring, dull, lifeless, and ugly— dressing in a sack and keeping every bit of skin covered. Now I know that modesty is humility. It's adorning oneself in a way that reflects the beauty and humility of Jesus. It starts with the heart. No matter how much skin you may cover up, if your heart isn't humble, you're not really being modest.—Claire, age 18

I ask myself if God would be proud of me if we were hanging out that day and this is what I showed up wearing. If He wouldn't be proud of me, then I'm probably not being modest.—Emily, age 16

Modesty is about dignity as a daughter of the King. As Princesses of our Heavenly Father we should act, talk, and dress like heaven.—Claire, age 18

Wily Woman

22

Have you ever seen that Looney Tunes cartoon in which Wile E. Coyote endlessly tries to catch the Road Runner?

As you've probably figured out, the coyote's name, "Wile E.", is a play on phonics for the word "wily." Wile E. Coyote is a wily coyote. He's always dreaming up new ways to catch the bird. "Wily" means crafty, cunning, sly, devious, or calculating. It includes using subtle tricks and schemes to get what you want.

And that description fits the Wild Thing to a "T"! The story in Proverbs 7 says, "Behold, the woman meets him, dressed as a prostitute, wily of heart" (Proverbs 7:10).

A Wild Thing is calculating. She's "wily of heart." Relying on her "wiles" is the approach she takes to relationships. She uses all sorts of schemes to catch and control the guy.

The Hebrew word translated "wily" means "guarded or secret." The phrase conveys the idea of a girl who has an underlying personal agenda. The corresponding Greek term means, "ready to do anything," usually in the bad sense of tricky and cunning behavior.

The wily girl:

- Has a personal agenda.

- Wants a man to satisfy it.

- Does whatever is necessary to make that happen.

> Trust in the LORD with all your heart, and do not lean on your own understanding. In all your ways acknowledge him, and he will make straight your paths.
>
> PROVERBS 3:5–6

Her number one aim is to get the guy to do what she wants. Her number one tactic is to secretly and skillfully pull his strings to get him to dance to her tune. She wants to write the script. She wants to sit in the director's chair.

The most famous biblical example of a wily woman is Delilah. She pulled Samson's strings like crazy. She teased, pouted, cried, gave him the cold shoulder, nagged, and schemed to get him to do what she wanted (Judges 16–17).

Manipulation falls into five basic categories:

···

- Sexual Manipulation—using your sexuality to charm the guy to do what you want, or using physical affection as a punishment or reward.

- Verbal Manipulation—nagging, lecturing, accusing, begging, and verbally bombarding the guy until he agrees to do things your way.

- Emotional Manipulation—playing on a guy's emotions by crying, pouting, sulking, withdrawing, or trying to make him feel guilty, insecure, or jealous.

- Spiritual Manipulation—telling him that you prayed about it and know what God wants him to do, or inappropriately spiritualizing the situation.

- Circumstantial Manipulation—plotting and arranging circumstances in order to direct the guy's behavior. (For example, pretending to sprain your ankle so that he has to hold or carry you.)

A wily approach to relationships trains a girl to develop the instincts of a hunter. Her foxy manipulations fill her heart with "snares" and "nets." The only way she knows how to get and keep a guy's attention is to entrap him. Unfortunately, when the guy clues in (which he inevitably does) he begins to view the relationship as a fate "more bitter than death" (Ecclesiastes 7:26), and the relationship breaks down.

Worse than that, manipulation dishonors God. It's near the top of the list of things He absolutely hates (Proverbs 6:16–19).

A Wise Thing takes a different approach to relationships—a radically different approach. She knows that the purpose of every relationship is God's glory, so she doesn't play the manipulation game. She gets off the director's chair and patiently trusts God to orchestrate her life's script.

Time FOR you

Time to READ

Ecclesiastes 7:26 ■ Job 5:12–14
■ Proverbs 3:5–6

Time to THINK

How does a wise one approach to relationships differ from a wily one?

What outcome awaits girls who use a wily approach?

What does the Lord promise those who trust Him with their love stories?

Time to PRAY

Pray Proverbs 3:5–6 over your love life. Resolve to trust the Lord with your future. Ask Him to help you avoid the sin of manipulation.

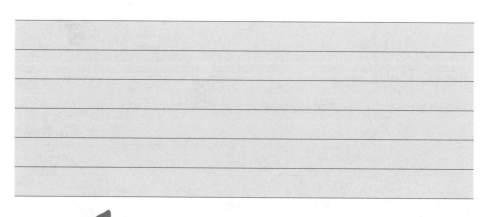

Time to LIVE FOR GOD'S GLORY

Over the next few years, the world will feed you a generous amount of advice on what you need to do in order to attract, snag, and keep a guy—how to bait the hook, cast the line, and reel him in.

Even if you're too young to be in a relationship right now, you can still resolve never to use a wily approach to control guys.

Think about your current friendships. Evaluate whether you are trying to control your friends, or whether you are trusting God to enable you to show them the goodness of His glory.

That Girl's Got Attitude

23

T he storyteller in Proverbs 7 uses two little words to describe the attitude of a typical Wild Thing:

"She is loud and wayward . . . " (Proverbs 7:11).

The phrase "loud and wayward" definitely describes a Wild Thing's behavior, but more than that, it sums up her prevailing state of mind. She's a sassy, defiant, my-way-or-the-highway kind of a girl. Nowadays, the dad might have described her by saying, "That girl has attitude!"

> But let your adorning be the hidden person of the heart with the imperishable beauty of a gentle and quiet spirit, which in God's sight is very precious. For this is how the holy women who hoped in God used to adorn themselves, by submitting to their own husbands.
>
> 1 PETER 3:4–5

- Loud is not so much the volume of her voice, although it definitely can include that. It's her insolence. This girl is sassy, brash, cheeky, flippant, mouthy, and pushy. She insists on her own way.

- Wayward means "to be stubborn and rebellious." It reflects a defiant, obstinate, nobody-tells-me-what-to-do frame of mind. The Wild Thing isn't open to input. She refuses to be led—especially by a man. Nobody tells her what to do!

If the Wild Thing of Proverbs 7 were alive today, she'd fit right in. In fact, she'd probably make it to the cover of *Cosmopolitan*, or be a candidate for a woman of the year award, or be featured in the who's who of the *Forbes* "Most Powerful Women" list, or maybe be hired by Hollywood to be the next sexy, aggressive, karate-chopping, gun-slinging, male-kicking female star.

Society preaches that a clamorous, defiant attitude for women is a virtue. Oh, it often dresses it up nicely and calls it something that makes it sound a bit more respectable—like self-confidence, assertiveness, or girl power—but it's really the same thing.

A strident, rebellious attitude stands in marked contrast to the soft, receptive demeanor that the Lord intended for women. Did you know that God created women with a uniquely feminine disposition?

When Adam first saw the woman, he broke into an exuberant, spontaneous poem. He said, "This at last is bone of my bones and flesh of my flesh; she shall be called Woman, because she was taken out of Man" (Genesis 2:23).

The original text of this scripture uses the word *Isha* for woman, and *ish* for man. The two words have a complementary meaning. *Ish* comes from the root meaning "strength" while *Isha* comes from the root meaning "soft." Isn't that fascinating?

The woman is the beautiful "soft" one—the receiver, responder, and relater. The life-giver.

The beautiful softness of womanhood was severely damaged when Eve sinned, but the New Testament directs us to reclaim the beauty of our original created design.

The New Testament talks about the imperishable beauty of a gentle and quiet womanly spirit. It also talks about amenability, agreeability, or deference—a willingness to respond that expresses itself in a married woman's life by her submission toward her husband, and in an unmarried woman's life in her willingness to respond and relate to others in a feminine manner.

Scripture teaches that softness is foundational to godly womanhood (1 Peter 3:4–5). Softness is not

Q. **Does submission mean that men are the bosses—and women have to do everything they say?**

A. No. The Bible directs a wife to submit herself to her husband, not to men in general. What's more, a wife is to submit "as to the Lord." In other words, her obedience to God comes first. Though she maintains a soft, agreeable, feminine disposition, she firmly says "no" to anything that goes against God's standards.

weakness. It involves having the wisdom, strength, and willpower to respond to the right things and in the right way. As Susan pointed out in the first section, the Lord wants His daughters to be strong "pillars" of grace.

When it comes to attitude, you have a choice to make. Will you accept the deceptive lie that is so prevalent in our culture—that a sassy, defiant spirit is desirable? And that a soft, receptive, agreeable disposition is a mark of weakness? Will you hang on to sin's twisted distortion of what it means to be a woman? Or will you agree with God about what kind of attitude is truly beautiful and precious in His sight?

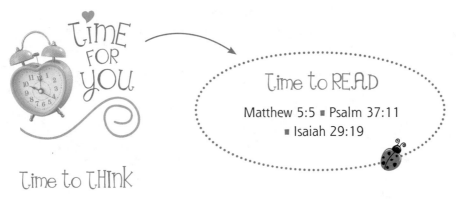

Time for you

Time to READ

Matthew 5:5 ▪ Psalm 37:11 ▪ Isaiah 29:19

Time to THINK

"Meek" is another word for "gentle." What does Scripture say are the benefits of cultivating this kind of disposition?

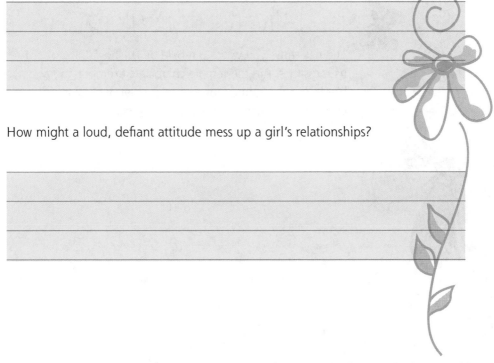

How might a loud, defiant attitude mess up a girl's relationships?

Why would some girls react negatively to the idea of being gentle, quiet, and agreeable?

_____

_____

_____

Are you more loud and defiant, or more gentle, quiet, and agreeable?
What can you do to cultivate more of the type of disposition that God wants?

_____

_____

_____

Time to PRAY

Pray a prayer based on 1 Peter 3:4. Ask the Lord to give you the imperishable beauty of a gentle and quiet spirit, which in God's sight is very precious.

Time to LIVE FOR GOD'S GLORY

The next time you watch a movie or TV show, think about its messages. Are the female characters exemplifying a sassy, brash, defiant attitude, or a gentle, quiet one? Would the Lord evaluate their attitude as "very precious"?

The media encourages girls to be loud and bossy. In shows, the quiet girl is always picked on and ridiculed.—Connie Jean, age 13

The world looks down on a woman with a "quiet" spirit.—Jenna, age 14

Femininity gets a bad rap, for sure. Our culture has made girls react to the idea of femininity like to the smell of sharp vinegar. My generation thinks that to be feminine is to be frumpy, old-fashioned, and boring. They think that a feminine woman is like the housewife of the 50s who is under her husband's thumb and does nothing but clean bathrooms and bottoms.—RuthAnne, age 17

In our society, a woman who makes a career and name for herself is looked upon with more favor than one who stays home and supports her family. A loud, demanding, arguing woman is looked upon with more favor than a joyful, gentle, compassionate one. We try to compete with the guys and prove ourselves to be just as rough, tough, and competent. We've lost the joy of behaving like women and fulfilling the role God intended for us.—Allison, age 17

Some girls would worry, I think, that having a gentle and quiet spirit means that they have to repress themselves and their personality and that they shouldn't speak up or ever be assertive.—Jacqueline, age 17

Femininity is often misrepresented as something it's not. Many women hate being a woman. Their version of femininity is drab and dowdy, feeling inhibited, being trampled by men. To them, femininity isn't something to be celebrated, but just a bunch of restrictive rules. One of the things that helped me to be feminine was seeing strong women who delighted in being who God has called them to be.—Claire, age 18

Many picture a "gentle and quiet" spirit as weakness, a suppression of their personality. However, I believe this spirit is found in a determined commitment and submission to the plan God has for your life. It doesn't mean losing your personality, but graciously submitting that personality to the plan of God. A woman who has a spirit quietly surrendered to the will of God is much more powerful than any woman who is trying to demand her rights.—Allison, age 17

Out and About

Did you know that "working at home" is on the Bible's Top Ten list of important things that older women need to teach the younger ones to do (Titus 2:5)?

It's quite countercultural to be talking about women being at home. Does that mean girls are the ones who should do all the cooking, laundry, cleaning, and child care? Does it mean that they shouldn't pursue education or careers or interests outside of the home?

Before we get to that, let's look back at the story of the Wild Thing of Proverbs 7. She provides the contrast to a girl who lives wisely. The storyteller tells us: "Her feet do not stay at home; now in the street, now in the market, and at every corner she lies in wait" (Proverbs 7:11–12).

"Now at the mall, now at the club, now at the movie theater, now at the party, now at the game" is how he could have described her behavior today.

He was trying to convey the point that the Wild Thing spent her time frequenting places where people gathered. She was constantly out and about. She wanted to be where the action was. She wanted to be amused and entertained, to have fun, and to feed her appetite for attention and admiration.

The problem was not so much that this young woman went out, but that she went out at the expense of what she should have been doing.

Her house was probably messy, her chores undone, her mail unopened, her bills unpaid, her exam unstudied for, her pantry unfilled, and her supper unmade. What's more, she probably

> She looks well to the ways of her household and does not eat the bread of idleness.
>
> PROVERBS 31:27

couldn't even remember the last time she read or studied her Bible or picked up a good, instructive Christian book.

Her priorities were out of order.

The habits of a Wise Thing are very different from the Wild Thing. Both are busy. But they are busy with different things. The Wild Thing is busy indulging herself. She is constantly out and about, looking for a good time. And she neglects things on the home front.

The girl who is wise attends to her private life first. Her habits are self-disciplined, self-sacrificing, and directed by the needs of her family.

Our home is our private sanctum. It's the "place"—physically and spiritually—where the most important stuff in life happens.

Having feet that "stay at home" has more to do with a woman's focus than her actual physical location. The wise woman of Proverbs 31 obviously went to the marketplace on a regular basis. She managed her own small business, supplying linen goods to the merchants. She was also involved in kingdom business, ministering to the poor and needy. But even though she physically went out of the home to do these things, she still maintained the right priorities—she looked well to the affairs of her household.

The world tempts us to think that all the important, exciting stuff happens "out there." But the Bible teaches that the most crucial matters of life happen from the inside out.

The Lord wants you to cherish and cultivate those things that HE regards as most important. And that's something you can start to do right now. You can develop a heart for the home by pitching in and helping your mom around the house, by making an effort to learn homemaking skills, by helping your family, by respecting your parents, and by making sure you've got all your priorities in the right order.

A Wild Thing is always out and about. But a Wise Thing curtails her social activity. She doesn't neglect her private, unseen life and her personal responsibilities. She is careful to put first things first.

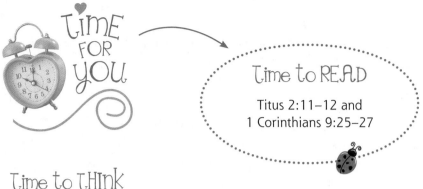

Time For You

Time to READ

Titus 2:11–12 and
1 Corinthians 9:25–27

Time to THINK

Why do you think the Lord wants to train you to live a self-controlled life?

Why is it tempting for girls to neglect their private, unseen lives and personal responsibilities?

Are you constantly out and about, or are you putting first things first?
What habits do you need to adjust to get your priorities in the right order?

Time to PRAY

Aren't you glad that the Lord gives you His Spirit to help? Write out a prayer based on 2 Timothy 1:7, asking the Lord to help you have the courage, discipline, and power to put first things first.

Time to LIVE FOR GOD'S GLORY

What's a home-based priority you've neglected? Do you need to clean your room? Iron some laundry? Help a sibling? Study for a test?

Today, do the thing you know you should do, but have been putting off. Ask the Holy Spirit to train you to live a self-controlled life.

On the Prowl

25

Have you ever watched a cat on the prowl?

My family has a tabby named "Miss Kitty" (the kids couldn't agree on a name). We also have a big, mild-mannered black lab dog, General Beau. The difference between them is quite entertaining.

> She opens her hand to the poor and reaches out her hands to the needy.
>
> PROVERBS 31:20

Our dog largely ignores our cat. But our cat will crouch and hide around a corner or on a chair—eyes alert, tail flicking— and then she'll pounce at Beau when he walks past. Out of the blue, she'll blitz across the room and whack him on the snout. Why? Because cats are natural predators. They're always on the lookout for a good hunt. They derive pleasure from prowling, pouncing, chasing, and entrapping.

The sage father of Proverbs likened a Wild Thing to a predator. He advised his son that this kind of woman "lies in wait": "Her feet do not stay at home; now in the street, now in the market, and at every corner she lies in wait" (Proverbs 7:11–12).

In the last lesson, we talked about the fact that the Wild Thing is always out and about because she gets a thrill from being on the prowl. Like my cat, she gets the evening crazies.

A Wild Thing lies in wait, focused on what she can get. She particularly wants to get the guy. Have you ever met a girl who's on the prowl to catch one?

Lying-in-wait behavior isn't restricted to getting a guy. It extends to getting other things too. Many women spend their whole lives lying in wait. They perpetually wait and watch for their next big catch, and hope that it will bring them the fulfillment they so desperately desire.

A Wild Thing "lies in wait" because she relies on other people and other things to satisfy her desires.

The wise father warned his son against getting caught in her trap. If the father had written his proverbs for a daughter, I'm sure he would have warned her against becoming a Wild Thing, because ultimately, the predator is just as susceptible to getting hurt as the prey.

The trap of a girl who lies in wait doesn't just snag the guy. It also entangles *her*. Scripture makes it clear that predators are trapped by their own devices. Their very own snares trip them up and destroy them. Psalm 9:16 tells us,

> "The wicked are snared in the
> work of their own hands."

The predatory behavior of a Wild Thing stands in marked contrast to the productive behavior of a Wise Thing. A wise girl doesn't waste time "lying in wait" for guys. She's too busy putting first things first. Time is too precious. There's far too much to be done and accomplished for Jesus.

She has a *kingdom* focus instead of a *me* focus. She's far more concerned about what she can give than what she can get. Her life is all about enjoying God and making Him famous. Giving, rather than getting, commands her attention.

Are you focused on giving—"opening your hand to the poor, reaching out your hands to the needy," and impacting the lives of those around you with the good news of the gospel of Jesus Christ?

The world encourages women to lie in wait for guys. But if you're smart, you'll ditch that focus and ask the Lord what He would like you to do today for His kingdom.

> **A wise girl doesn't waste time "lying in wait" for guys.** She's too busy putting first things first. Time is too precious. There's far too much to be done and accomplished for Jesus.

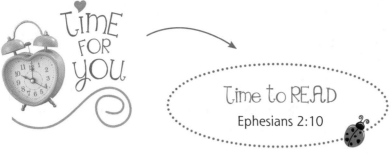

Time to THINK

Make a list of things you'd like to have. (Material things and things like friends, attention, etc.)

How might lying in wait for these things interfere with the good works God has prepared for you to do?

What's your focus? You can usually tell by evaluating what you spend the most time thinking about. Do you spend most of your time and energy thinking about how to get or how to give?

How can you shift your focus from "getting" to "giving"?

Time to PRAY

Write out a prayer based on Proverbs 31:20, asking the Lord to help you open your heart and hands to the needs of those around you.

_____

_____

_____

_____

_____

Time to LIVE FOR GOD'S GLORY

What "good work" does God want you to do today? Ask Him to show you. Keep your eyes open for someone who could use your help or encouragement. Later, write down how He had you open your hands and reach out to someone in need.

_____

_____

_____

_____

_____

Role Reversal

26

nowadays, women are encouraged to be the aggressors, pursuers, and initiators in male and female relationships. More often than not, the girls take charge and push the relationship along.

> But now, O LORD, you are our Father; we are the clay, and you are our potter; we are all the work of your hand.
>
> ISAIAH 64:8

Taking the lead is exactly what the Wild Thing in Proverbs 7 did.

If she would have had an iPhone, I'm sure she would have bombarded the young man with text messages and aggressively monitored and posted on his Facebook page. She would have been the one who initiated contact and arranged dates. She would have been the one who picked him up and dropped him off.

The storyteller points out that *she* was the one who "seizes him"... And *he* ended up following *her*.

"She seizes him . . . he follows her." (Proverbs 7:13, 22)

So what's wrong with that?

According to the Bible, this pattern goes against God's design.

I know that it's promoted in our culture. But it doesn't honor who God created women to be. And in my experience, relationships based on this pattern end up in dysfunction and disappointment, and often in complete disaster.

You see, when God created male and female, He provided an object lesson—a visible testimony—to His entire plan of redemption (Ephesians 5).

History started with God creating a man and a woman and uniting them as husband and wife because it will end with the marriage and spiritual union of Christ the bridegroom and His Bride, the Church.

God had the *end* in mind before the beginning. He had the marriage and union of Christ and the Church in mind when He created gender.

Manhood, womanhood, marriage, and sex are images that exist for the express purpose of pointing us to something else. They are mini lessons that tell the amazing story of the gospel!

They're like a movie trailer, giving us a glimpse into the epic love story of the Bridegroom who made a covenant commitment to His Bride . . .

- How He loves her so much that He gave up everything to be with Her.

- How He faithfully pursues Her.

- How He's exclusively and wholeheartedly committed to Her.

- How She loves Him.

- How She makes herself beautiful for Him.

- How She longs for Him.

- How She remains faithful to Him.

- How She prepares for their wedding.

- How happy and amazing their union will one day be.

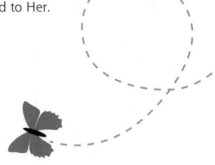

This cosmic love story is so magnificent that God chose to put it on display permanently. Everywhere. Men were created to reflect the strength, love, and initiatory self-sacrifice of Christ. Women were created to reflect the character, grace, beauty, and responsiveness of the Bride He redeemed.

Imagine that! Your womanhood was created to tell the spectacular story of what a love relationship with Jesus is all about!

You were created to display the story of the gospel in a way that only a woman can. Males were created to display the story of the gospel in a way that only a man can.

That doesn't mean you have to be a girly girl, like the color pink, and fuss when you break a nail. Or that you can't like sports, cars, or building things. Womanhood isn't about fitting a certain stereotype.

But it does mean that in your relationships with guys, you respect God's design.

When God created male and female, He provided an object lesson—a visible testimony—to His entire plan of redemption.

Time FOR you

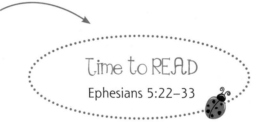

Time to READ
Ephesians 5:22–33

Time to THINK

According to Ephesians 5:32, to what mystery does the union of man and woman in marriage point?

How are male and female roles in marriage supposed to reflect the relationship between Christ and the Church?

Based on this pattern, what characteristics should you look for in a guy before you consider marrying him?

Time to PRAY

Write a prayer based on Isaiah 64:8, acknowledging that God is the potter and you are the clay. Ask Him to help shape you into the woman He wants you to be.

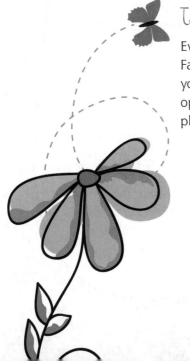

Time to LIVE FOR GOD'S GLORY

Evaluate whether you are in the habit of constantly texting, Facebooking, and pursuing guys. Do you need to restrain yourself? You can be a life-giver by providing guys with the opportunity and supporting their efforts to step up to the plate and become the men God wants them to be.

A mom shows care and love. Not that a dad doesn't... it's just that a mom has that more "tender" side. Dads are the protectors.—Elisha, age 13

Women are more compassionate and have a nurturing quality that men do not have nor cannot teach boys to have. Men have a protective and provider instinct that cannot be taught by a woman.—RuthAnne, age 17

Guys are action oriented. Girls are emotion oriented. We think about and feel things. They do things. It's just two different ways of thinking. Neither is better than the other. We need each other to make up for our strengths and weaknesses. —Montana, age 18

Both male and female are created in God's image and showcase different aspects of who He is. In marriage the husband shows Christ's sacrificial leadership for the Church and His tireless pursuit of Her. The wife, on the other hand, shows Christ's submission to the Father and the way that the Holy Spirit serves the Church as a Helper.—Jacqueline, age 17

If the relationship doesn't start with the man taking the initiative, will he take the initiative after marriage? I don't think so. This also ruins the picture. Relationships are supposed to reflect Christ and His Bride. Marriage is first and foremost about God. When we honor His design and plan, He will honor us.—Claire, age 18

Although occasionally I think, "Hey, that's not fair, I should be able to do that too!" most of the time I am very glad that God created different gender roles. I like being a woman. When I was younger I used to totally fight against any insinuation that being a woman was different from being a man, and I would look down on anything that I perceived as feminine or "girly." But as I grew older, God worked on my heart. I started to like being a girl. It almost brought me a sense of relief because I realized I could just be who God designed me to be. I think the relief came because I stopped fighting the natural order and yielded to God's plan. It's important that gender roles as designed by God not be confused with gender roles as prescribed by our culture. I don't think it goes against God's design for a girl to be athletic or to gravitate toward traditionally male-dominated areas—by liking math, science, or cars, for example.— Jacqueline, age 17

27

messing Around

T he Proverbs 7 story is about a young married woman who got entangled in a relationship with a single guy. Her husband is out of town. So she leaves her condo and heads out for a prearranged rendezvous with her love interest. She's dressed provocatively. She flirts with him. And then she gets things rolling by pulling him close and kissing him. Proverbs 7:13 says, "She seizes him and kisses him."

> For this is the will of God . . . that each one of you know how to control his own body in holiness and honor . . . that no one transgress and wrong his brother in this matter . . . For God has not called us for impurity, but in holiness.
>
> 1 THESSALONIANS 4:3–7

Most people would disapprove of her conduct. They would say a married woman kissing a man other than her husband is wrong. Even most wild celebrities would agree with that.

But what if we were to change the story line up a bit? What if this Wild Thing of Proverbs had been single?

In that case, would kissing the young man have been wrong? What if she engaged in increasingly deeper forms of sexual intimacy with him? What if she invited him over to her condo, and they fondled each other and made out in all sorts of ways? At what point would her behavior cross the line?

"How far is too far?" is a question many Christians wrestle with. But I think it's the wrong question. In my mind, we can't hope to get our sexual conduct right until we understand what sex is all about.

Why did God create sex? What's the purpose of it? I asked that question on Facebook, Twitter, and out on the street. Here are the answers I got:

- To express love

- To bond

- To experience intimacy

- To make babies

- To have fun

All those answers are true at some level. But none are the primary reason. I want to give you a short phrase that I think wraps the biblical reason for sex. Are you ready? Here it is:

To tell the story

Why does sex exist? To tell the story. Which story? *The* big story. The Story of Christ's covenant relationship with His Bride.

The covenant part is important. What's a covenant? A covenant is a binding, legal agreement between two parties. The cup we drink at communion represents "the New Covenant"—that is, the agreement Christ established on the cross. His covenant "legally" pays the price for our sin and allows us to enter into a relationship with Him.

The covenant opens the door for intimacy and union. We can't be one with Christ until we accept the terms of His covenant.

Marriage and sex are supposed to mirror this spiritual reality. The legal covenant comes

Q. **Why does the Bible restrict sex to marriage?**

A. Sex confirms a husband's and wife's covenant union. It physically testifies that a spiritual, supernatural, and legal joining has taken place. That's why God restricts sex to marriage. If unmarried individuals have sex, they tell a lie with their bodies. They testify that a covenant has taken place, when in fact it hasn't.

first. Sexual intimacy follows. A couple's sexual union physically illustrates that a legal union has taken place. It's an amazing physical image that the two have become one.

So what does that mean for sexual conduct outside of marriage? The simple answer is that it's wrong for two people to act as if they are married when they are not married—you don't sleep together, you don't have sleepovers, you don't live together, you don't spend all your time together, you don't mess around. You save expressions of physical intimacy for marriage.

A girl who wants to glorify God will aim to have her sexual behavior mirror the purity and faithfulness of Christ's Bride to her one and only Groom.

How far is too far is really the wrong question. A much better one for you to ask yourself is this:

How well does my sexual conduct tell the gospel Story?

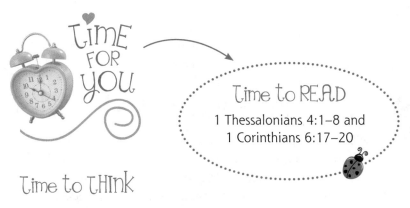

Time FOR YOU

Time to READ
1 Thessalonians 4:1–8 and
1 Corinthians 6:17–20

Time to THINK

In your own words, define "sexual purity."

Using the passages you just read, list some reasons why it's important for you to pursue holiness in your sexual conduct.

How does sexual purity glorify God?

Time to PRAY

Use 1 Thessalonians 4:1 to pray. Ask the Lord to help you please Him with your sexual conduct. Pray that you might do so more and more.

Time to LIVE FOR GOD'S GLORY

Because we live in a sexually impure world, sexual purity is an ongoing challenge. Are there any impure thoughts, actions, or habits you need to confess? Talk to a friend, mentor, youth leader, or parent. Ask them to keep you accountable. And don't forget that because of the new covenant, you are forgiven. God's grace covers all your sin!

Get It from the Girls . . .

There's a lot of pressure on girls to become sexually active. They hear all their friends are doing it.—Elisha, age 13

Everyone I know is either in a relationship or looking for one. Most of them are younger than me! This is a negative trend because a nine-year-old is not ready to be looking for a husband! If a girl gives in to the pressure to get a boyfriend, then she could give in to the pressure of kissing or giving away her virginity.—Connie Jean, age 13

Sex is all around us and everyone is doing it. Pressure is even coming from within the church. Many Christians think purity isn't a big deal. Young women are constantly being told these lies.—Claire, age 18

Our culture sends the message that sex outside of marriage is so normal that you're weird if you don't want to participate. The media often portrays older virgins as people with mental retardation, OCD, nerds, or else extremely ignorant about sex and basic biology. There is pressure to become sexually active to avoid being thought of as any of those things.—Jacqueline, age 17

God gives us this gift called sex to share with one person for our whole life, because when we open this gift and use it we are joined to the other person: mind, heart, and body. If we break up there is no way to avoid the pain and sadness that will come from opening the gift too early. God asks us to wait because He doesn't want us to have that type of hurt to deal with.—Morgan, age 16

Sexual purity is saving yourself for your husband. Because if you have sex before you're married you will get attached spiritually to that person.—Connie Jean, age 13

Sexual purity means saving not only your body, but also your mind and heart for marriage.—Morgan, age 16

"Sexual purity" is so much more than not having sex outside of marriage. It's a lifestyle of godliness and purity. To be pure in heart, mind, and body. All equally important.—RuthAnne, age 17

I wish, especially in youth groups, that there would be less lessons of "Don't have sex" and more of "This is what God designed for a man and wife." I think a lot of young people today in Christian circles misunderstand sex.—Montana, age 18

28

Breaking Curfews

Years ago I took my kids on a day trip on an old steam train. At one crossing we saw two big tanker trucks approaching. We noticed with concern that the driver of the first truck wasn't slowing down like he should. He was driving as though the warning lights, clanging bells, and train weren't there.

> The prudent sees danger and hides himself, but the simple go on and suffer for it.
>
> PROVERBS 22:3

To our horror, he didn't stop. He kept driving and crashed into the back of the train. His truck crumpled like a flimsy aluminum can and rolled into the ditch. We were all jolted and thrown down, but uninjured. The truck driver wasn't so fortunate. He was seriously hurt.

Everyone was perplexed about why the driver didn't pay attention to the boundary. Didn't he see the warning lights? Didn't he hear the clanging bells? Didn't he know he could get hurt? Why didn't he stop?

Like that truck at the railway crossing, a Wild Thing disregards boundaries.

The young woman of Proverbs 7 almost certainly didn't begin her marriage planning to commit adultery. But bit by bit she got to that point. One small compromise led to another until finally, she ended up in an immoral situation that she would have never envisioned at the start.

The storyteller tells us that she met the young man late at night, "in the twilight, in the evening, at the time of night and darkness" (Proverbs 7:9).

He implies that there was something inappropriate about her heading out at that time. In being out that late, under the cover of darkness, alone, without her husband, her behavior crossed the boundary from appropriate to inappropriate.

You couldn't exactly call it sin—there are no "Thou shall not go out alone after midnight" directives in the Bible. But it was definitely unwise. It opened the door to sin. If she would have had a policy about not hanging out alone on dark streets she wouldn't have continued down the track of compromise.

After she crossed the first boundary of going out late at night, and the second boundary of secretly meeting a man, she crossed the boundary of appropriate touch by kissing him. She crossed another boundary when she engaged in inappropriate flattery and flirtation, and another when she invited him over to her place. Before she knew it, she had violated all the boundaries that would have kept her safe.

She ignored the flashing lights and warning bells and drove headlong into a relationship that was going to end in disaster and a heart-load of hurt.

It always amazes me when I see women foolishly putting themselves in vulnerable situations. The wise father asked, "Can a man carry fire next to his chest and his clothes not be burned? Or can one walk on hot coals and his feet not be scorched?" (Proverbs 6:27–28).

When you're young your parents set protective boundaries for you. But as you get older you'll need to establish some personal rules for yourself.

For example, you may decide that you will not go out with a mixed group of boys and girls without a parent present; or that you will not study alone with a guy in a secluded place; that you will not meet a guy alone at Starbucks; or that you will not allow a boy to text you unless he has met your parents.

> **Wise girls** don't put themselves in situations that increase the risk of sin. They see the danger and put up boundaries to avoid it.

Time FOR you

Time to READ
Proverbs 14:16 and 27:12

Time to THINK

Have you set up personal rules to safeguard your purity? In the space below, make a list of some wise boundaries. Knowing what your boundaries are ahead of time will help guide you when you encounter potentially compromising situations.

Time to PRAY

Pray Proverbs 22:3. Ask the Lord to help you see danger and hide from it. Ask Him to help you observe the boundaries that will keep you safe.

Time to LIVE FOR GOD'S GLORY

Discuss your list with your mom, mentor, friend, or female youth leader. Ask for feedback and suggestions. Make a commitment to abide by your personal rules. Boundaries are only helpful if you observe them.

Boundaries can get frustrating, but they keep you out of trouble. Once you actually get rid of those boundaries, you wonder why you actually WANTED to get rid of them!
—Connie Jean, age 13

I think that parents set these boundaries to protect their kids. I never used to like them, but I obeyed them when I was younger. As I got older I liked them even less and started to bend and break them. Now that I have been able to see what has happened because I broke those rules, I realize they are for my good and can follow them.—Emily, age 16

I am grateful that my parents care enough to give me boundaries. They established them because they love me, care about me, and don't want me to get hurt.—Rebecca, age 16

As I get older I can see where my parents' rules protected me in huge ways as a young teenager and child. It's their wisdom and we need to respect it.
—RuthAnne, age 17

My parents have put boundaries in place for my protection. Many of my friends who did not submit to boundaries their parents had in place are now living miserable lives in bondage to sin. Those girls could have easily been me if I had chosen not to accept the protection and training of my parents.—Allison, age 17

Most rules parents make are for our own good and are logical. If you don't understand one, ask! I didn't understand sometimes when I committed what I considered a minor infraction. But after talking it over I often realized that there was a bigger issue (lack of communication, responsibility, trust) underneath the simple rule.—Montana, age 18

Smoking, drinking, getting addicted to illegal drugs, getting pregnant, and getting an abortion . . . there are TONS of examples of girls getting in trouble because they didn't like boundaries!—Connie Jean, age 13

Set boundaries in your heart and head as well. Don't let your brain go to places it shouldn't and pour Scripture into your heart that will guide and correct you when you stray. Boundaries are necessary because of Jeremiah 17:9. Our hearts are deceitful and can't be trusted, so we have to be the watchmen and always be on guard for the enemy.—RuthAnne, age 17

29

Two-Faced

Can you guess where the Wild Thing went before she arrived at the rendezvous point to seduce the young man? It wasn't to the mall, the gym, or the beauty salon.

She went to church.

Yep. On the day they met up, the Wild Thing went to the temple to offer a sacrifice to God: "She seizes him and kisses him, and with bold face she says to him, "I had to offer sacrifices, and today I have paid my vows" (Proverbs 7:13–14).

Jewish people made vow offerings to express their gratitude to God. The giver took a meat sacrifice and loaves of freshly baked bread, pastries, and cakes to the temple. Some of the offering was burned on the altar, some was given to the priests, and the remaining food was taken home for a celebratory meal.

Since the meal was holy, the guests had to go through washing rituals and be ceremonially holy in order to partake. They had to clean themselves up, wash their clothes, and dress up for the occasion.

The whole process symbolized the intent of the guests to be spiritually "clean" so they could fellowship with their holy God.

The Wild Thing's vow sacrifice was clearly a farce. She only put on the "Good Girl" act to keep people from seeing the "Bad Girl" underneath. She had no intention of being good. She was planning to sin.

> Whoever walks in integrity walks securely, but he who makes his ways crooked will be found out.
>
> PROVERBS 10:9

She actually used the holy meal as a ploy to get the young man over to her house and into her bed. She was a two-faced hypocrite. A pretender.

A hypocrite pretends to be very good or religious when she's aware she is not. She puts on an act to impress people. She play-acts at loving God.

The Bible is very clear that the Lord can't stand it when people "talk the talk" but don't "walk the walk." In other words, when they pretend to be religious, but intentionally keep sinning. God told some pretenders: "Bring no more vain offerings . . . I cannot endure iniquity and solemn assembly . . . your appointed feasts my soul hates; they have become a burden to me . . . I will hide my eyes from you; even though you make many prayers, I will not listen! . . . Wash yourselves; make yourselves clean; remove the evil of your deeds from before my eyes; cease to do evil, learn to do good" (Isaiah 1:13–17).

Jesus couldn't tolerate religious hypocrisy either. He said, "Woe to you, scribes and Pharisees, hypocrites! For you are like whitewashed tombs, which outwardly appear beautiful, but within are full of dead people's bones and all uncleanness. So you also outwardly appear righteous to others, but within you are full of hypocrisy and lawlessness" (Matthew 23:27–28).

For the Lord, an unrepentant heart and religious behavior just don't mix.

A Wise Thing relies on the power of the Holy Spirit to help her keep the inner, hidden parts of her life just as pure as the outer, visible ones. She avoids wearing masks. Who she is in public is the same as who she is in private. She's honest about her struggle with sin, and does not try to hide.

"Hypocrite" comes from the Greek word for an actor in a stage play. In ancient Greek comedies and tragedies, the actors wore masks to represent the character they were playing. The mask projected the desired image. Hiding their true selves behind a mask is what hypocrites do.

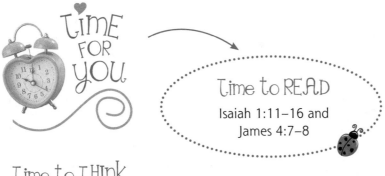

TIME FOR YOU

Time to READ
Isaiah 1:11–16 and
James 4:7–8

Time to THINK

Why is hypocrisy unhealthy and dangerous?

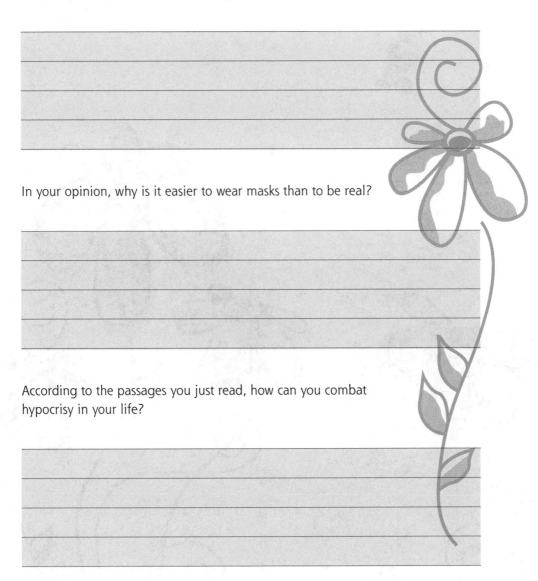

In your opinion, why is it easier to wear masks than to be real?

According to the passages you just read, how can you combat hypocrisy in your life?

Time to PRAY

Pray James 4:7–8.

Time to LIVE FOR GOD'S GLORY

Are you covering up sin and pretending to be someone you are not? Share your struggles with a sister, a mentor, your mom, or a trusted friend. Have her pray with you. It may be tough, but bringing sin out into the open is a powerful way to help you overcome it.

30

Clingy Girl

My girlfriend Jan had to give away her young Labradoodle dog because it was far too needy. It clung to her far too much.

The Labradoodle could not bear to be parted. It wouldn't go outside to relieve itself unless Jan went along. In the house it would always be right beside her—pressed against Jan's leg. If Jan took a shower, the Labradoodle would sit crying, with its back against the shower door. If she tried to leave the house, the dog would throw itself into a frenzy and near cardiac arrest.

As a deer pants for flowing streams, so pants my soul for you, O God. My soul thirsts for God, for the living God.

PSALM 42:1–2

The neediness of Jan's Labradoodle illustrates a common characteristic of a Wild Thing: She desperately clings to relationships, looking to others for affirmation.

As the Proverbs 7 narrative unfolds, we see the woman expressing her hope that the young man will come to her house and meet her needs. She says, "So now I have come out to meet you, to seek you eagerly, and I have found you" (Proverbs 7:15).

She strokes the young man's ego by emphasizing his importance to her: "I have come out to meet *you*. *You* are the man of my dreams! *You* are so amazing, so strong, so handsome, so right for me! *You* are the only one who can make me happy! I'm so glad that I found *you*!"

She puffs up his head to think that he is the only one who can rescue her from her loveless plight. He's her knight in shining armor, her savior. But the truth is, her flattery has very little to do with him being sensational and very much to do with her being needy.

We've all seen clingy girls. They cling to guys, desperately looking to them to validate them.

A passage in Jeremiah speaks to those who try to quench their neediness through human relationships. It warns that doing so will not satisfy:

"Cursed is the man who trusts in man and makes flesh his strength, whose heart turns away from the Lord. He is like a shrub in the desert, and shall not see any good come. He shall dwell in the parched places of the wilderness, in an uninhabited salt land. Blessed is the man who trusts in the Lord, whose trust is the Lord. He is like a tree planted by water, that sends out its roots by the stream, and does not fear when heat comes, for its leaves remain green, and is not anxious in the year of drought, for it does not cease to bear fruit" (Jeremiah 17:5–8).

If a girl relies on people to meet all her needs, she'll be left "thirsting." But if she looks to the Lord, she'll be like a tree planted by water. Her leaves will remain green—even if her human relationships go through dry spells.

Though marriage is a great gift, no man on the face of earth can ever fill the God-shaped vacuum in a woman's heart. Nor can any other relationship. A Wise Thing doesn't depend on people for her happiness or sense of self. Instead, she delights in the Lord, and looks to Him to satisfy her soul-thirst.

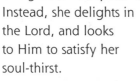

"All my life I had a longing
For a drink from some clear spring,
That I hoped would quench the burning
Of the thirst I felt within.
Hallelujah! I have found Him
Whom my soul so long has craved!
Jesus satisfies my longing,
Through His blood I now am saved."

"Satisfied" by Clara T. Williams

Time FOR YOU

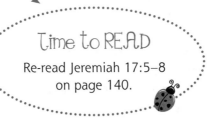

Time to READ

Re-read Jeremiah 17:5–8 on page 140.

Time to THINK

Use Jeremiah 17:5–8 to compare and contrast the characteristics of a woman who depends on man with a woman who depends on the Lord:

"She who depends on man . . ."   **"but she who depends on the Lord . . ."**

Time to PRAY

Write out a prayer based on Psalm 42:1–2, expressing your soul-thirst for the Lord.

Time to LIVE FOR GOD'S GLORY

Are you a clingy girl? Take an honest look at your life. To whom or what are you currently looking to meet the deep desires of your heart? Are you hanging on too tight? Always remember that Jesus is the only one who can truly satisfy your soul-thirst.

Get It from the Girls . . .

The world sends out the message through movies and music that to be happy, you need to be in love or "having fun" with a boy. When teen girls see this, like in a romance movie or something, they start to want it, and I think that's a huge part of what is driving girls to become boy crazy.—Emily, age 16

A girl's friends, the movies she watches, and the books she reads, can contribute to her going "boy crazy." Many girls train their minds to dwell on the wrong things. Also, many lack a strong attachment to their fathers, and I think this contributes to their boy craziness. A girl can avoid getting caught up in boy craziness by letting Christ be her all in all. It's easier said than done, but it's not impossible.—RuthAnne, age 17

Loneliness, low self-worth, lack of identity, and a bad dad (or parents) can contribute to girls becoming boy crazy. Many girls look to guys to affirm their worth, and to receive the love and attention they didn't get at home. Hard or unsatisfying circumstances may also cause a girl to obsess about guys. She turns to him as a way of escape.—Claire, age 18

When a girl is too focused on a guy it can consume her. It's hard for her to think about what God wants her to do.—Allison, age 14

Focus on a boyfriend can be stressful and upsetting. It takes your focus off of God, family, friends, and school.—Erica, age 15

How can a girl avoid getting caught up in boy craziness? Realize that Jesus is the best guy you can EVER have a relationship with. You're His princess. What could be better?—Montana, age 18

I feel like I have a message to share: "Girls, stop looking to guys for affirmation and love—because God is waiting to supply it all!" I had to look in the mirror day after day to convince myself of this. I had to pray constantly to get over my lust, my desire for love, and my thinking that a guy would fulfill me. But I went through that fire. And now I'm here. I assure you if you give everything to God you won't be disappointed.—Savannah, age 16

Shopaholic

31

As we rejoin the story of our Proverbs 7 woman, we see that she tries to heighten the young man's interest by describing the luxurious, designer décor in her bedroom. She says, "I have spread my couch with coverings, colored linens from Egyptian linen; I have perfumed my bed with myrrh, aloes, and cinnamon" (Proverbs 7:16–17).

> Do not lay up for yourselves treasures on earth, where moth and rust destroy and where thieves break in and steal, but lay up for yourselves treasures in heaven, where neither moth nor rust destroys and where thieves do not break in and steal. For where your treasure is, there your heart will be also.
>
> MATTHEW 6:19–21

The type of bed she described was an impractical extravagance that very few people could afford. She wanted to let the guy know that she didn't sleep on a pallet on the floor like a lowly commoner. Her bed was a couch. It was a luxury item.

She also made sure to mention that she had spread her bed with coverings of delicate cushions, and with linens imported from Egypt. Egyptian linen was the top-of-the-line, designer brand. It was the finest and most desirable cloth in the world.

I'm sure the young man thought, *Wow!* His eyebrows probably rose even farther when he heard that she had perfumed her linens with imported, exotic, pricey fragrances. She made it clear that she spared no expense in preparing for their night of romance.

The fact that the Wild Thing took such care to describe her possessions gives us a clue as to her attitude toward them.

She was a shopaholic who loved designer brands!

Heading down to the mall to go shopping was probably one of her favorite pastimes. She was obsessed with spending her time and money on things that would indulge her senses, and that would make others desire or envy her.

The attitude of a wise woman toward her possessions is markedly different. "She opens her hand to the poor and reaches out her hands to the needy . . . all her household are clothed in scarlet. She makes bed coverings for herself; her clothing is fine linen and purple" (Proverbs 31:20–22).

The Proverbs 31 woman ensured that she and her family were dressed nicely, in quality clothing. She made wise, careful, financial decisions. But unlike her wild counterpart, she didn't brag about her possessions, nor did she obsess about owning the latest, greatest, designer brand. She likely could have afforded the pricey Egyptian linens. But she chose to forego the luxury, make her own bed coverings, and give money to the poor and needy instead.

A Wise Thing treasures Jesus more than she treasures the things of this world. She regards the work of the kingdom as more important than self-indulging. She rejects the popular consumer mindset. She seeks to invest her resources— money, time, talents, and gifts—in things that truly matter; in things that have eternal value.

The Bible teaches that what you do with money is important. The girl who makes material riches her goal in life—a shopaholic who constantly fills her closet with more and more stuff—has the wrong values. However prosperous she may appear, she is poverty-stricken in God's sight.

> **A Wise Thing** treasures Jesus more than she treasures the things of this world. She regards the work of the kingdom as more important than self-indulging.

The truly rich girl is the one whose main aim in life is to please the Lord, and who invests what He has given her to produce a return for God's kingdom.

If you invest in faith and good works— opening your hand to the poor and reaching out your hands to the needy, you will accumulate a heavenly bank balance that will last forever!

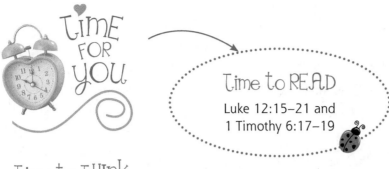

Time FOR you

Time to READ

Luke 12:15–21 and
1 Timothy 6:17–19

Time to THINK

What point was Jesus trying to make in the parable about the rich farmer?

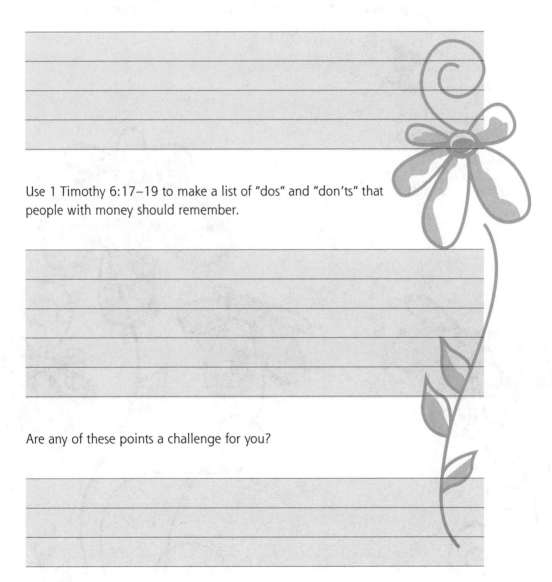

Use 1 Timothy 6:17–19 to make a list of "dos" and "don'ts" that people with money should remember.

Are any of these points a challenge for you?

Time to PRAY

Pray Matthew 6:19–21, asking the Lord to help you store up treasure in the right place.

Time to LIVE FOR GOD'S GLORY

Today, plan to use some of your resources—money, time, gifts, or talents—to build God's kingdom. Think about how you could open your hand to the poor or reach out your hand to the needy. Pray and ask the Lord what He would have you do.

lover of Pleasure

32

The Wild Thing had primped herself to look provocative, seductively kissed the young man, told him about the sumptuous food she had prepared, and described the lavish, sensual décor of her bedroom. She could tell he was tempted. Her subtle hints paved the way for her shameless proposition: "Come, let us take our fill of love till morning; let us delight ourselves with love" (Proverbs 7:18).

> And he said to all, "If anyone would come after me, let him deny himself and take up his cross daily and follow me. For whoever would save his life will lose it, but whoever loses his life for my sake will save it."
>
> LUKE 9:23–24

Essentially she urged him, "Let's indulge! Let's make love all night. Let's play and pleasure ourselves to the max."

She wanted to indulge in illicit sex. But it appears that she was in the habit of indulging in other things too. She indulged in her wardrobe, in designer brands, in food, in going out, in staying up late and sleeping in, and in neglecting her home. If she lived today, she'd have probably indulged in TV, movies, the Internet, gossip, beauty treatments, expensive restaurants, vacations, and buying all of the latest and greatest stuff.

A Wild Thing is intent on immediate gratification. Enjoyment, comfort, luxury, and ease are what she feels she deserves and what she constantly seeks and demands. Her attitude is: "I have a right to be happy! I deserve this!"

Though she thinks she's "living it up," the Lord's verdict is just the opposite. A girl who lives for pleasure may be physically alive, but spiritually, she is dead.

"She who is self-indulgent is dead even while she lives" (1 Timothy 5:6).

Jesus told His followers that if they truly wanted to live, they needed to follow His example of self-denial.

A girl who wants to experience all the joy and fullness of a relationship with Christ needs to deny herself and take up her cross daily and follow Him.

She must be willing to make sacrifices.

She must be willing to give up lesser joys for infinitely greater ones. On this side of heaven, Christian discipleship is a costly, uncomfortable, and painful business.

One of my favorite parables is the one about the pearl of great price: "The kingdom of heaven is like a merchant in search of fine pearls, who, on finding one pearl of great value, went and sold all that he had and bought it" (Matthew 13:45–46).

The merchant was so ecstatic about the prospect of getting the spectacular pearl that he gladly gave up everything else. It was worth more to him than the combined value of all his other possessions.

That story pretty much sums up the reason why we should be willing to deny self and suffer. It's not because discomfort and pain are enjoyable, but because the treasure we've set our hearts on is worth the cost. The sufferings of this present time are nothing compared with the glory that we will enjoy in Jesus.

Do you believe it? Do you believe that treasuring Christ holds greater pleasure than sex, wealth, power, and prestige? Are you willing to say "no" to the things the world says will make you happy and say "yes" to what the Lord says will make you happy? Are you willing to do what God asks of you, even if it isn't easy? Even if it hurts?

It will cost. For some, it will cost a great deal. But the price tag is nothing when compared to the incomparable value of that amazing pearl!

"They that deny themselves for Christ, shall enjoy themselves in Christ."
—John Mason

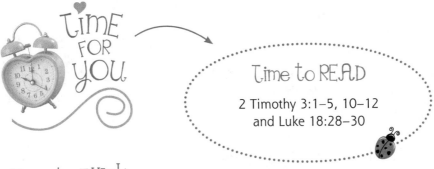

Time to THINK

Use 2 Timothy 3:2–4 to make a list of traits that are incompatible with godliness. Put a star beside the ones that you struggle with.

Verse 12 says, "All who desire to live a godly life . . . will be persecuted." If you try to live a godly life, what kind of persecution might you face?

What makes a person willing to walk the path of self-sacrifice?

Time to PRAY

Pray a prayer based on Luke 9:23–24. Ask the Lord to help you avoid becoming a "lover of pleasure." Ask Him for the strength to deny yourself and to take up your cross daily and follow Him.

Time to LIVE FOR GOD'S GLORY

What "cross" is the Lord asking you to carry today? Does He want you to forgive someone? Or repent? Or return good for evil? Or give up a habit? Or deny yourself a pleasure? Are you willing to part with the "pearl" to which you've been hanging on in order to gain The Pearl of Great Price?

Breaking Faith

33

The Wild Thing assured the young man that they wouldn't be caught; her husband was a merchant who often took long trips out of town: "For my husband is not at home; he has gone on a long journey; he took a bag of money with him; at full moon he will come home" (Proverbs 7:19–20).

The woman was in love when she got married (Proverbs 2:17). We don't know for sure what happened to change that. But whatever it was, I'm convinced she had a compelling reason to justify her behavior.

- Maybe she felt trapped in a loveless marriage.

- Maybe her husband was rude and inconsiderate.

- Maybe he was so busy in his business ventures and was away so much that she felt ignored, isolated, and lonely.

- Maybe she suspected that he had been unfaithful.

However she justified it, the bottom line is that *she* wasn't loyal to the promise *she* had made. She wasn't a woman of her word. When her husband was out of town, she cheated on him. She broke faith.

Faithfulness means that I do what I said I was going to do, even if it's hard for me to do it.

> The one who pursues righteousness and faithful love will find life, righteousness, and honor.
>
> PROVERBS 21:21 HCSB

Scripture emphasizes that faithfulness is an attribute of God. He always does what He says He's going to do. If He makes a promise, He keeps it. If He makes a commitment, He never turns His back on it. He's faithful to fulfill His responsibility and keep His word. He's totally and completely trustworthy. He doesn't back out—even when we don't keep our end of the bargain.

"If we are faithless, he remains faithful—for he cannot deny himself" (2 Timothy 2:13).

The Wild Thing was unfaithful to the solemn marriage promise she made. But breaking her promise didn't start the night she cheated on her husband. It started long before that.

She broke her promise when she was critical, when she snapped back, when she failed to forgive, when she harbored bitterness, when she withheld love, when she started to dream of being in another relationship . . . when she read that book and watched that movie.

A Wild Thing thinks that the little stuff isn't that important. It doesn't matter if she said she'd be there, and then wasn't—or if she said she'd do it, and then didn't. Or said she wouldn't, and then did. Or if she said she was in, and then backed out. What's the big deal?

But being faithful in little things is extremely important. Jesus said that a person who is faithful in little things is also faithful in big things; she who is unreliable in small, seemingly trivial commitments, will also be unreliable in big commitments.

Luke 16:10 tells us, "One who is faithful in a very little is also faithful in much, and one who is dishonest in a very little is also dishonest in much."

The best way for a girl to be faithful to a big commitment is to learn how to be faithful to little ones. And that starts long before she gets married.

The Pharisees had some silly rules. They argued that if you swore by the altar it was like having your fingers crossed behind your back, but if you swore by the offering on the altar, you had a duty to do what you said. Jesus told them to stop using oaths to indicate when they were telling the truth and simply tell the truth (see Matthew 5:34–37).

How about you? Are you a promise keeper? Are you reliable in the little things? Are you being faithful to your commitments? Do you do what you said you're going to do, even if it's hard for you to do it?

Have you followed through and done what you told your parent or a friend you would do?

A Wise Thing is a woman of her word. When she says she's going to do something, she faithfully follows through.

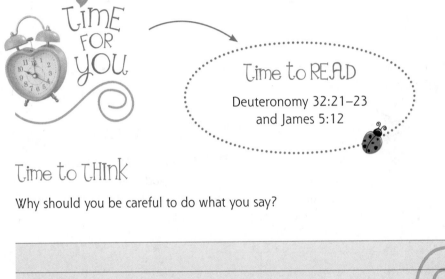

time For you

time to READ

Deuteronomy 32:21–23
and James 5:12

time to THINK

Why should you be careful to do what you say?

What do these verses teach about making rash or foolish commitments?

If a girlfriend breaks her word to you, does that justify you breaking your word to her? Why or why not? (Hint: Check out how Jesus responds to unfaithfulness in 2 Timothy 2:13.)

_____

_____

_____

_____

_____

Time to PRAY

Pray a prayer based on Proverbs 21:21. Ask the Lord to help you be as faithful to your commitments as He is to His.

Time to LIVE FOR GOD'S GLORY

Are you a promise keeper? Have you failed to follow through on a commitment? Today, do what you can to follow through on your commitment. Resolve to be careful about the commitments you make.

34

Bad Influence

The young man initially resisted the advances of the Wild Thing. He wasn't sure about getting entangled in a messy situation with a married woman. But then he gave in. She convinced him to sin: "With much seductive speech she persuades him; with her smooth talk she compels him. All at once he follows her, as an ox goes to the slaughter, or as a stag is caught fast till an arrow pierces its liver; as a bird rushes into a snare; he does not know that it will cost him his life" (Proverbs 7:21–23).

> Whoever walks with the wise becomes wise, but the companion of fools will suffer harm.
>
> PROVERBS 13:20

"Persuades" is translated from a Hebrew verb meaning "to bend or turn." It indicates that the woman turned the young man away from the direction in which he was headed.

She was the negative influence that compelled him to sin. That's not to say he wasn't responsible for his behavior. He was just as guilty as she was. But she was the bad influence—the fatal attraction—that put him on the crooked path that led to his downfall.

I wonder if the young man thought he was immune to her influence. I wonder if he rationalized that he'd just hang out for a short while and keep her company that evening. She was obviously lonely, unhappy with her marriage, and in desperate need of a friend.

Maybe he thought he could help her—maybe he thought he could be a positive influence. The fact that she had to persuade, compel, and sweet-talk, and that he hesitated before giving in, indicates that his standards for sexual conduct were higher than hers, and that he wasn't planning on having an affair.

Negative influence is very powerful. Not only does the Bible want us to stop being a negative influence on others, it also wants us to avoid people who might exert a negative influence on us. It warns:

"A righteous man is cautious in friendship, but the way of the wicked leads them astray" (Proverbs 12:26 NIV 1984).

If you constantly and exclusively hang out with people who don't love the Lord, chances are they'll have a greater influence on you than you'll have on them. They'll affect you negatively. As 1 Corinthians 15:33 warns us, "Do not be deceived: 'Bad company ruins good morals.'"

Wise girls won't take on just anyone as a friend. They look at a person's character. They know that friends are a powerful influence, so they choose them carefully.

Solomon warned his son to stay away from wild women. But sadly, later in life, he ended up going against his own advice. He started keeping the wrong kind of company. The women he associated with were a negative influence on him and turned his heart away from wholeheartedly following the Lord (1 Kings 11:9–10).

He was probably tripped by the classic, foolish assumption that "it won't happen to me."

I'm amazed at the number of girls who think they are immune to the power of negative influence. They think they're strong enough and smart enough to be above the threat. So they start taking foolish risks in relationships. They let down their defenses, cross boundaries, crash and burn—and then wonder how it all happened.

What kind of people are you hanging out with? Remember: "Whoever walks with the wise becomes wise, but the companion of fools will suffer harm."

Influence: the capacity or power of a person to be a compelling force on the actions, behavior, and opinions of others; to affect, sway, move, or induce. (From Latin *influere*—to flow into). When a driver is "under the influence," (DUI), his behavior is adversely affected by alcohol or other intoxicants. He's susceptible to dangerous errors in judgment and is at high risk for hurting himself and others. Sadly, the wrong friends can produce a similar effect. A girl who lives under their influence is also susceptible to dangerous errors in judgment and is at high risk for injury.

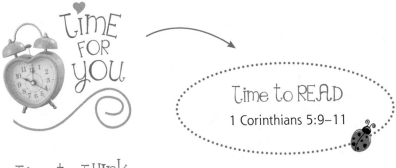

Time to READ

1 Corinthians 5:9–11

Time to THINK

What advice about friends did Paul give the believers in Corinth?

Why do you think Paul advised them not to hang out with hypocrites?

Can you think of an example of a friend or family member for whom bad company ruined good morals? Did that person think that his or her morals would be compromised?

Time to PRAY

Write out a prayer, personalizing Proverbs 13:20.

Time to LIVE FOR GOD'S GLORY

What kind of company do you keep? Do you need to establish deeper friendships with people who truly love Jesus? Are any of your friends exerting a negative influence on you? Do you need to pull back from constantly hanging out with them? Ask the Lord to help you walk with the wise and avoid being a companion of fools.

35

Going Wise

The young man falls for the seduction. He follows the Wild Thing home and they spend the night together. The "stolen water is sweet, and bread eaten in secret is pleasant," but the story doesn't have a happy ending (Proverbs 9:17).

> The ear that listens to life-giving reproof will dwell among the wise.
>
> PROVERBS 15:31

The storyteller wraps it up with the grim conclusion:

"Many a victim has she laid low, and all her slain are a mighty throng. Her house is the way to Sheol, going down to the chambers of death" (Proverbs 7:26–27).

The Wild Thing dishonors her God-given purpose. She fails to be a life-giver. She becomes a life-taker instead.

Maybe her husband finds out. Maybe she gets pregnant. Maybe the young man gets an STD. Maybe she loses her reputation. Maybe she breaks his heart. Maybe they get drawn deeper into sin. We don't know the details, but we do know that their behavior disrupts their relationship to God. It leads to spiritual death.

The naïve young man who lacked sense and the wily seductress who caused his downfall are both examples of individuals who lacked wisdom.

The book of Proverbs repeatedly talks about three types of individuals who turn their backs on God's wisdom: the simple, the fools, and the scoffers.

"How long, O simple ones, will you love being simple? How long will scoffers delight in their scoffing and fools hate knowledge?" (Proverbs 1:22).

The simple person is somewhat open to instruction; the fool, less so; and the scoffer, on the far end of the spectrum, is completely resistant and closed.

From the simple to the fool to the scoffer, there is an increasing hostility and resistance to learning and to doing things God's way. A Wild Thing will fall somewhere along this continuum. She will be like Simple Sally, Foolish Fran, or Scoffing Sue.

Simple Sally is the female version of the young man in our story. She's simple. Uninformed. She doesn't have the necessary life-experience or know-how. She doesn't see the danger, so she's easily taken in.

Sally is the girl who gets herself into trouble because she hangs out with the wrong friends, goes to the wrong places, takes the wrong advice, and makes bad choices. She wanders down the wrong path because she hasn't made the effort to learn, and therefore doesn't know any better.

Foolish Fran isn't uniformed. She knows better. She's heard the message of wisdom. But she's unconcerned. She just doesn't care. The thing that matters most to Fran is having fun. She thinks she has life figured out and under control. Fran doesn't take God seriously. She doesn't think that anything bad will happen. She thinks she'll be able to stop before she goes too far.

Lady Wise invites guests to come and dine (Proverbs 9:5–6):

Scoffing Sue retorts, "How dare you suggest my way is wrong?"

Foolish Fran replies, "No thanks. I've got it all figured out."

Simple Sally says, "Not right now. Maybe later."

But Wise Wendy affirms, "I'm on my way. I want to feast at your table!"

How will YOU respond to the invitation?

And then there's Scoffing Sue. While Sally is uninformed, and Fran is unconcerned, Sue is unashamed. Sue insists that God's way is wrong. She makes up her own rules. She doesn't care what God thinks, nor does she care what others have to say about it.

Simple Sally can't be bothered to listen to the Bible's wisdom for women, Foolish Fran doesn't see a reason to, and Scoffing Sue brashly refuses.

But unlike these three types of girls, the Wise Thing is teachable. She chooses to embrace wisdom and pattern her life according to God's divine design.

She seeks to become a true woman who thinks, prays, and lives for His glory.

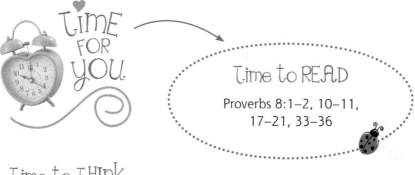

Time to READ
Proverbs 8:1–2, 10–11, 17–21, 33–36

Time to THINK

Can you identify a situation or time when you acted like Simple Sally, Foolish Fran, or Scoffing Sue?

According to verse 36, what will happen to girls who don't seek wisdom?

What does the Lord promise to those who to those who diligently seek wisdom?

Time to PRAY

Pray Proverbs 8:33–35 for your life.

Time to LIVE FOR GOD'S GLORY

Look back over all the devotions in this book. What have you learned about womanhood? As you go through life, make a habit of asking yourself "Am I behaving like a Wild Thing or like a Wise Thing?" Am I being a life-giver or a life-taker? Aim to constantly think, pray, and live for God's glory.

Get It from the Girls...

If we are thinking of what honors God, we will make decisions much differently. Instead of hanging out with that girl because she's popular, we'd sit with the girl who just moved to our town and share Jesus with her. When we seek to glorify God in all we do, we will become His woman... a woman who loves yet fears Him and who seeks to please Him in everything she does. It's a high calling and one worth fighting for.—RuthAnne, age 17

I've had a wonderful example of how to live for God's glory from a friend I met in my freshman year of high school. Her passion for Christ was obvious in everything she did. She loved to talk about Him. She made it her mission in life to show others the love of Christ and she did it, not by waiting to be a missionary in a foreign country, but by smiling. If you were having a tough day, or looked a little down, she'd give you a beautiful smile, and your day could instantly turn around. Sadly, my friend died. I want to honor her life by honoring God, because that is what she did every day. I had always wanted to do something "big," something life changing for the Lord. I wanted to save a nation, or start a huge organization. I didn't know how to glorify God in the little things. Now, because of my friend's amazing life, and even her death, I know that I can glorify God simply by smiling, or helping someone in the hallway, by standing up for someone when they're being bullied, or by giving them a hug when they're having a hard day.—Hannah, age 14

*Desiring to live for the glory of God has definitely impacted me and my decisions as a high school and college student. I've realized that I can glorify God as a single, that I don't need a boyfriend. I've realized that I can glorify God through my relationships with other people, loving and encouraging them as Christ did to the people He met. I've realized that I can glorify God through my schoolwork, being diligent and dedicated to the task God has given me at this time. Living for God takes the focus off of me and what I want and onto God and what He wants. Basically, to glorify God is to show everyone else how awesome He is and how marvelous are the works of His hands!
—Montana, age 18*

Well Girls,

You've come to the end of this devotional. We pray that you'll continue to put the things you've learned into practice and hope you'll come back to read and refer to this material often. We've only scratched the surface of what it means to be God's True Woman. Figuring out womanhood will be a journey for you, as it has been—and still is—for us.

The material in Part 1 of this book was drawn from a three-year discipleship program for teen girls that Susan wrote for Sunday school classes and small groups, entitled TRUE: Becoming a True Woman, published by the Presbyterian Church in America Christian Education Committee.

The material in Part 2 of this book was drawn from Mary's book and Bible study entitled, *Girls Gone Wise—in a World Gone Wild*, published by Moody Publishers.

They're both great resources that can help you go deeper and understand more about God's incredible design.

In closing, we just want you to know how much we love your generation! We are so proud and excited to witness a movement of courageous, countercultural young women rising up to stand strong against the tide of popular opinion, to put God's glory on display.

Because in the end, that's what womanhood is all about.

It's not about us. It's meant to shine the spotlight on God's amazing plan of redemption through Jesus.

Your longings for love, affirmation, acceptance, beauty, romance, intimacy, connection, family, and belonging—all the deep longings of a girl's heart—ultimately point to a relationship with Jesus. You may or may not ever get married. But if you accept Christ's proposal, you can participate in the eternal, heavenly marriage covenant to which the earthly marriage covenant points. Christ will fulfill your every longing.

Have you said "yes" to Jesus? Have you made the commitment to love, honor, and obey Him?

We pray that you have. And that you will continue on this life-long journey of becoming God's True Woman!

Love,

Susan & Mary

A Glossary

Atone: to make things right again. Everything was wrong between God and the people He had created. Because the people were constantly guilty of sin, they could not share close relationship with a holy, perfect Creator. And people, being sinful, couldn't make things right by themselves. But God offered a loving solution: Jesus, who was perfect, would pay the price for our sins and make things right between God and people. Because of Jesus, we can have right relationship with God again!

Covenant: a sacred, binding promise between two people. Marriage is a covenant. God made a covenant with Abraham that He would be faithful to His chosen people (the Israelites). God's "new covenant" promises His faithfulness to all Christ-followers.

Elect: those who are chosen by God to be His followers. God chose His people before the foundation of the world, and it is God who draws people to Himself.

Glory: the wonderful splendor of God's great honor. Until we get to heaven, we can't really understand God's glory. But we praise the awesome holiness and majesty of God (respecting His glory) and we try to behave in ways that make others glimpse that holy majesty (glorifying God with our lives).

Grace: God's goodness to us that we don't earn or deserve at all. God loves and forgives us because He is so awesome and because Jesus gave His life for us. We show grace to others by sharing God's goodness and love, even when they don't deserve it, either.

Holy/Holiness: perfectly free from sin. Only God is truly holy, but the perfect sinlessness of Jesus becomes ours when we become Christ-followers. We ask for God's Holy Spirit to help us live up to the holiness that God already sees when He looks at us.

Redemption: being set free from bondage because someone paid the ransom. No person except Jesus could live up to God's standards for holy living, so we were like slaves to sin. But Jesus paid the ransom when He died for us on the Cross. Now we are not slaves but God's own family.

Repent: to turn away from sin. Repentance goes way beyond feeling sorry that we did what doesn't please God; repentance seeks to make a big change and leave that sin behind.

Righteousness: perfect moral purity. Only God is truly righteous, but if we are Christians, we claim Christ's righteousness as our own. God sees us as righteous, and we try to live righteously, like Jesus.

Salvation: being rescued from the effects of sin because Jesus paid our penalty on the Cross. No one can earn salvation; it is a free gift from God.

Sanctification: being set apart for a sacred purpose, purified from sin. Christ's people are already set apart as God's own, but He keeps on working to clear away our old habits of sinfulness so that we can glorify God and live for Him.

Sin: anything that goes against God's law or God's will. The Bible tells us what pleases God with instructions such as the two greatest commandments—to love God and to love other people. Sin is choosing our own way instead of God's ways. God loved us and saved us, even while we were still sinners.

Sovereignty: God's right to do whatever He wants with His creation. God has authority and power over all that He has made, including our lives. A king is sometimes called a "sovereign," but no earthly king is sovereign over God's sovereignty!

Hypocrisy: pretending in your outward words and actions to be what you really aren't on the inside. You can fool people with smart or spiritual-sounding words and good deeds, but God sees right to your heart and knows when you obey Him out of love for Him.

Wisdom: thinking and decision-making based on God's standards of what's right and wrong. For Christ-followers, wisdom is more than just knowledge or good judgment. It's a regular pattern of choosing God's way rather than foolish ways.

A true wöman BOOK

The goal of the **True Woman** publishing line is to encourage women to:

- *Discover, embrace, and delight in God's divine design and mission for their lives*
- *Reflect the beauty and heart of Jesus Christ to their world*
- *Intentionally pass the baton of Truth on to the next generation*
- *Pray earnestly for an outpouring of God's Spirit in their families, churches, nation and world*

To learn more about the **True Woman movement** and the many resources available for individuals, small groups, and local church women's ministries, visit us online:

- *www.ReviveOurHearts.com*
- *www.TrueWoman.com*
- *www.LiesYoungWomenBelieve.com*

The **True Woman Manifesto** summarizes the core beliefs at the heart of this movement. You can sign the manifesto, find a downloadable PDF, and order additional copies at:

- *www.Truewoman.com/Manifesto*

True Woman is an outreach of:

Revive Our Hearts

Calling women to freedom, fullness, and fruitfulness in Christ

P.O. Box 2000 | Niles, MI 49120

A true wöman BOOK

MORE RESOURCES ...

**Girls Gone Wise
Paperback**

**Girls Gone Wise
DVD**

**Girls Gone Wise
Group Study Kit**

Includes book, study
guide, and DVD

... FOR GIRLS GONE WISE

You'll find videos, a forum, and many other resources to
help you learn how to walk wisely on the GirlsGoneWise.com
website. And make sure to follow *Girls Gone Wise* on
Facebook (facebook.com/girlgonewise) and
Twitter (twitter.com/girlsgonewise) too!

**Also available, *Girls Gone Wise* gear!
Get the bag, mug, and buttons.**

Becoming a
TRUE Woman

Who is teaching our teen and pre-teen girls what it means to be a woman—the church or the culture? The cultural message about womanhood is delivered visually and verbally 24/7. This resource will help the family and church disciple teen girls in biblical principles of womanhood.

Visit www.myTrueTeen.com
for more information, sample chapters, FAQ, and pricing
Or call 1-800-283-1357 to speak with a product representative